flavours of thailand

70 easy authentic recipes

MARKS & SPENCER

PLEASE NOTE that the cup and spoon
measurements used in this book are metric.
A conversion chart appears on page 126.

This edition first published in 2008 by
ACP Magazines Ltd
Exclusively for Marks and Spencer plc

www.marksandspencer.com

First published 2008
Copyright ACP Magazines Ltd 2008

ISBN: 978-1-903777-18-3

Printed and bound in China

contents

money bags tung tong

1 tablespoon peanut oil
1 small brown onion (80g),
chopped finely
1 clove garlic, crushed
1 tablespoon grated fresh ginger
100g chicken mince
1 tablespoon finely grated
palm sugar
1 tablespoon finely chopped
roasted unsalted peanuts
2 teaspoons finely chopped
fresh coriander
3 spring onions
24 x 8cm-square wonton wrappers
vegetable oil, for deep-frying

PEANUT DIPPING SAUCE
1 tablespoon peanut oil
2 cloves garlic, crushed
1 small brown onion (80g),
chopped finely
2 fresh small red chillies,
deseeded, chopped coarsely
1 stick fresh lemon grass,
chopped finely
3/4 cup (180ml) coconut milk
2 tablespoons fish sauce
1/4 cup firmly packed dark
brown sugar
1/2 cup (140g) crunchy
peanut butter
1/2 teaspoon curry powder
1 tablespoon lime juice

1 Heat oil in wok; stir-fry onion, garlic and ginger until onion softens. Add chicken; stir-fry until chicken is changed in colour. Add sugar; stir-fry about 3 minutes or until sugar dissolves. Stir nuts and coriander into filling mixture.
2 Cut upper green half of each spring onion into four long slices; discard remaining white half. Submerge onion strips in hot water for a few seconds to make pliable.
3 Place 12 wrappers on board; cover each wrapper with another, placed on the diagonal to form star shape. Place rounded teaspoons of the filling mixture in centre of each star; gather corners to form pouch shape. Tie spring onion strip around neck of each pouch to hold closed, secure with toothpick.
4 Make dipping sauce (freeze excess for a future use).
5 Just before serving, heat oil in wok or large saucepan; deep-fry money bags, in batches, until crisp and browned lightly. Drain on absorbent paper; serve with peanut dipping sauce.

PEANUT DIPPING SAUCE Heat oil in small saucepan; cook garlic and onion until softened. Stir in remaining ingredients; bring to a boil. Reduce heat; simmer, stirring, about 2 minutes or until sauce thickens.

MAKES 12 MONEY BAGS AND 1½ CUPS DIPPING SAUCE
PER MONEY BAG 5.1G FAT; 425KJ (101 CAL)
PER TABLESPOON DIPPING SAUCE 7G FAT; 378KJ (90 CAL)

spring rolls poh pia tod

PREPARATION TIME 20 MINUTES COOKING TIME 20 MINUTES
(PLUS REFRIGERATION TIME)

20g rice vermicelli
2 teaspoons peanut oil
100g pork mince
1 clove garlic, crushed
1 fresh small red thai chilli, chopped finely
1 spring onion, chopped finely
1 small carrot (70g), grated finely
1 teaspoon finely chopped coriander
root and stem mixture
1 teaspoon fish sauce
50g shelled cooked prawns, chopped finely
1 teaspoon cornflour
2 teaspoons water
12 x 12cm-square spring roll wrappers
vegetable oil, for deep-frying

CUCUMBER DIPPING SAUCE
1 cucumber, deseeded, sliced thinly
1/2 cup (110g) sugar
1 cup (250ml) water
1/2 cup (125ml) white vinegar
1 tablespoon grated fresh ginger
1 teaspoon salt
2 fresh small red thai chillies, sliced thinly
3 spring onions, sliced thinly
1 tablespoon coarsely chopped
fresh coriander

1 Place vermicelli in medium heatproof bowl; cover with boiling water. Stand until just tender; drain. Using kitchen scissors, cut vermicelli into random lengths.

2 Heat oil in wok; stir-fry pork, garlic and chilli until pork is changed in colour. Add onion, carrot, coriander mixture, fish sauce and prawns; stir-fry until vegetables just soften. Place stir-fried mixture in small bowl with vermicelli; cool.

3 Blend cornflour with the water in small bowl. Place 1 level table-spoon of the filling near one corner of each wrapper. Lightly brush edges of each wrapper with cornflour mixture; roll to enclose filling, folding in ends.

4 Make dipping sauce (freeze excess for a future use).

5 Just before serving, heat oil in wok or large saucepan; deep-fry spring rolls, in batches, until golden brown. Drain on absorbent paper; serve with cucumber dipping sauce.

CUCUMBER DIPPING SAUCE Place cucumber in heatproof serving bowl. Combine sugar, the water, vinegar, ginger and salt in small saucepan, stir over heat without boiling until sugar is dissolved; pour over cucumber. Sprinkle with chilli, onion and coriander; r efrigerate, covered, until chilled.

MAKES 12 SPRING ROLLS AND 1½ CUPS DIPPING SAUCE
PER SPRING ROLL 3.5G FAT; 279KJ (67 CAL)
PER TABLESPOON DIPPING SAUCE 0G FAT; 107KJ (26 CAL)

starters & soups

7

curry puffs   kari puff

PREPARATION TIME 30 MINUTES   COOKING TIME 35 MINUTES

2 teaspoons peanut oil
2 teaspoons finely chopped
coriander root
2 spring onions, chopped finely
1 clove garlic, crushed
100g beef mince
1/2 teaspoon ground turmeric
1/2 teaspoon ground cumin
1/4 teaspoon ground coriander
2 teaspoons fish sauce
1 tablespoon water
1/2 cup (110g) mashed potato
2 sheets ready-rolled frozen
puff pastry
1 egg, beaten lightly
vegetable oil, for deep frying

SWEET CHILLI DIPPING SAUCE
12 fresh small red thai chillies,
chopped coarsely
8 cloves garlic, quartered
2 cups (500ml) white vinegar
1 cup (220g) caster sugar
2 teaspoons salt
2 teaspoons tamarind paste

1 Make dipping sauce (freeze excess for a future use).
2 Heat oil in wok; stir-fry coriander root, onion, garlic and beef until beef is changed in colour. Add turmeric, cumin and ground coriander; stir-fry until fragrant. Add fish sauce and the water; simmer, uncovered, until mixture thickens. Stir in potato; cool.
3 Using 9cm cutter, cut four rounds from each pastry sheet. Place 1 level tablespoon of the filling in centre of each round; brush around edge lightly with egg. Fold pastry over to enclose filling, pressing edges together to seal.
4 Just before serving, heat oil in large saucepan; deep-fry curry puffs, in batches, until crisp and browned lightly. Drain on absorbent paper; serve with dipping sauce.

SWEET CHILLI DIPPING SAUCE Place ingredients in medium saucepan, stir over heat without boiling until sugar is dissolved; bring to a boil. Reduce heat; simmer, uncovered, about 20 minutes or until slightly thickened. Cool 5 minutes; blend or process until pureed.

MAKES 8 CURRY PUFFS AND 1½ CUPS DIPPING SAUCE
PER CURRY PUFF 8.3G FAT; 481KJ (115 CAL)
PER TABLESPOON DIPPING SAUCE 0G FAT; 220KJ (52 CAL)

mixed satay sticks satay gai, nuah, muu

PREPARATION TIME 20 MINUTES (PLUS MARINATING TIME)
COOKING TIME 15 MINUTES

250g chicken breast fillets
250g beef eye fillet
250g pork fillet
2 cloves garlic, crushed
2 teaspoons brown sugar
$1/4$ teaspoon sambal oelek
1 teaspoon ground turmeric
$1/4$ teaspoon curry powder
$1/2$ teaspoon ground cumin
$1/2$ teaspoon ground coriander
2 tablespoons peanut oil

SATAY SAUCE

$1/2$ cup (80g) roasted unsalted peanuts
2 tablespoons red curry paste (page 121)
$3/4$ cup (180ml) coconut milk
$1/4$ cup (60ml) chicken stock
1 tablespoon kaffir lime juice
1 tablespoon brown sugar

1 Cut chicken, beef and pork into long 1.5cm-thick strips; thread strips onto skewers. Place skewers, in single layer, on tray or in shallow baking dish; brush with combined garlic, sugar, sambal, spices and oil. Cover; refrigerate 3 hours or overnight.
2 Make satay sauce.
3 Cook skewers on heated oiled grill plate (or grill or barbecue) until browned all over and cooked as desired. Serve immediately with satay sauce.

SATAY SAUCE Blend or process nuts until chopped finely; add paste, process until just combined. Bring coconut milk to a boil in small saucepan; add peanut mixture, whisking until smooth. Reduce heat, add stock; cook, stirring, about 3 minutes or until sauce thickens slightly. Add juice and sugar, stirring, until sugar dissolves.

MAKES 12 SKEWERS AND 1¼ CUPS SATAY SAUCE
PER SKEWER 6.1G FAT; 471KJ (112 CAL)
PER TABLESPOON SATAY SAUCE 5.5G FAT; 278KJ (66 CAL)

TIP If using wooden skewers, soak well in cold water before preparing.

lime and coconut prawns

PREPARATION TIME 15 MINUTES (PLUS REFRIGERATION TIME)
COOKING TIME 15 MINUTES

24 uncooked medium
king prawns (1kg)
$1/3$ cup (80ml) lime juice
$1/2$ cup (125ml) coconut milk
$1/2$ cup (75g) plain flour
$1^1/2$ cups (100g) shredded coconut
peanut oil, for deep-frying

PEANUT DIPPING SAUCE
$1/3$ cup (50g) toasted unsalted
peanuts
$1/3$ cup (80ml) lime juice
$1/4$ cup (60ml) chicken stock
$1/4$ cup (60ml) coconut milk
2 tablespoons smooth peanut butter
1 tablespoon sweet chilli sauce

1 Shell and devein prawns, leaving tails intact. Combine juice and coconut milk in medium bowl; add prawns, toss to coat in marinade. Cover; refrigerate 1 hour.
2 Meanwhile, make peanut dipping sauce.
3 Drain prawns; reserve marinade. Holding prawns by tail, coat in flour then reserved marinade, then in coconut. Heat oil in wok; deep-fry prawns, in batches, until brown. Drain. Serve with warm sauce.

PEANUT DIPPING SAUCE Combine nuts, juice, stock and coconut milk in small saucepan; bring to a boil. Reduce heat; simmer, uncovered, 5 minutes. Blend or process with peanut butter and sauce until smooth.

MAKES 24
PER PRAWN 8.6G FAT; 485KJ (116 CAL)

honey and orange prawns

PREPARATION TIME 15 MINUTES (PLUS REFRIGERATION TIME)
COOKING TIME 10 MINUTES

24 uncooked medium king prawns (1kg)
2 teaspoons olive oil
1 teaspoon finely grated orange rind
2 tablespoons orange juice
2 tablespoons honey

SOY GINGER DIP
$^1/_3$ cup (80ml) soy sauce
2 teaspoons white sugar
1cm piece fresh ginger (5g), grated

1 Shell and devein prawns, leaving tails intact. Combine oil, rind, juice and half of the honey in medium bowl; add prawns, toss to coat in marinade. Cover; refrigerate 1 hour.
2 Meanwhile, combine ingredients for soy ginger dip in small saucepan; stir over low heat until sugar dissolves.
3 Cook drained prawns, in batches, on heated oiled grill plate (or grill or barbecue), brushing with remaining honey, until just changed in colour.
4 Serve prawns with warm dip.

MAKES 24
PER PRAWN 0.5G FAT; 134KJ (32 CAL)

fish cakes tod mun pla

PREPARATION TIME 15 MINUTES   COOKING TIME 10 MINUTES

500g redfish fillets, skinned and boned
2 tablespoons red curry paste
(page 121)
2 fresh kaffir lime leaves, torn
2 spring onions, chopped coarsely
1 tablespoon fish sauce
1 tablespoon lime juice
2 tablespoons finely chopped
fresh coriander
3 snake beans (30g), chopped finely
2 fresh small red thai chillies,
chopped finely
peanut oil, for deep-frying

1 Cut fish into small pieces. Blend or process fish with curry paste, lime leaves, onion, sauce and juice until mixture forms a smooth paste. Combine fish mixture in medium bowl with coriander, beans and chilli.

2 Roll heaped tablespoon of the fish mixture into ball, then flatten into cake shape; repeat with remaining mixture.

3 Just before serving, heat oil in wok or large saucepan; deep-fry fish cakes, in batches, until browned lightly and cooked through. Drain on absorbent paper; serve with fresh coriander leaves and lime wedges, if desired.

MAKES 16 FISH CAKES
PER FISH CAKE 2.8G FAT; 201KJ (48 CAL)

crying tiger   seur rong hai

PREPARATION TIME 20 MINUTES (PLUS MARINATING TIME)
COOKING TIME 10 MINUTES (PLUS STANDING TIME)

50g dried tamarind
1 cup (250ml) boiling water
400g beef eye fillet
2 cloves garlic, crushed
2 teaspoons dried green
peppercorns, crushed
1 tablespoon peanut oil
2 tablespoons fish sauce
2 tablespoons soy sauce
1 stick fresh lemon grass,
chopped finely
2 fresh small red thai chillies,
chopped finely
1 large carrot (180g)
1 cup (80g) thinly sliced
chinese cabbage

CRYING TIGER SAUCE
$1/4$ cup (60ml) fish sauce
$1/4$ cup (60ml) lime juice
2 teaspoons grated palm sugar
1 teaspoon finely chopped
dried red thai chilli
1 spring onion, sliced thinly
2 teaspoons finely chopped
fresh coriander
reserved tamarind pulp
(see step 1)

1 Soak tamarind in the water for 30 minutes. Pour tamarind into a fine strainer set over a small bowl; push as much tamarind pulp through the strainer as possible, scraping underside of strainer occasionally. Discard any tamarind solids left in strainer; reserve $1/2$ cup of pulp for the crying tiger sauce.

2 Halve beef lengthways. Combine remaining tamarind pulp, garlic, peppercorns, oil, sauces, lemon grass and chilli in large bowl; add beef, stir to coat beef all over in marinade. Cover; refrigerate 3 hours or overnight.

3 Make crying tiger sauce.

4 Cook beef on heated oiled grill plate (or grill or barbecue) about 10 minutes or until browned all over and cooked as desired. Cover beef; stand 10 minutes, slice thinly.

5 Meanwhile, cut carrot into 10cm lengths; slice each length thinly, cut slices into thin matchsticks.

6 Place sliced beef on serving dish with carrot and cabbage; serve crying tiger sauce separately.

CRYING TIGER SAUCE Combine ingredients in small bowl; whisk until sugar dissolves.

SERVES 4
PER SERVING 10.9G FAT; 951KJ (227 CAL)

starters & soups

17

spicy seafood soup   poh taek

PREPARATION TIME 20 MINUTES
COOKING TIME 15 MINUTES

1 medium uncooked blue swimmer crab (500g)
150g firm white fish fillets
8 medium black mussels (200g)
150g squid hoods
1.25 litres (5 cups) chicken stock
2 sticks fresh lemon grass, chopped finely
20g piece fresh galangal, sliced thinly
4 fresh kaffir lime leaves
6 fresh small green thai chillies, chopped coarsely
4 dried long red thai chillies, chopped finely
8 large uncooked prawns (400g)
1 teaspoon grated palm sugar
2 tablespoons fish sauce
1 tablespoon lime juice
1/4 cup fresh thai basil leaves

1 Remove and discard back shell and gills of crab;
rinse under cold water. Chop crab body into
quarters, leaving claws intact. Cut fish into bite-
sized portions; scrub mussels, remove beards.
Cut squid into 2cm-thick slices; score the inside in
a diagonal pattern.
2 Combine chicken stock, lemon grass, galangal,
lime leaves and both chillies in large saucepan;
bring to a boil.
3 Add prepared seafood and unshelled prawns
to boiling stock mixture; cook, uncovered, about
5 minutes or until seafood is just cooked through.
Remove from heat; stir in remaining ingredients.
Serve hot.

SERVES 4
PER SERVING 2.8G FAT; 815KJ (195 CAL)

chicken and galangal soup   tom ka gai

PREPARATION TIME 15 MINUTES (PLUS STANDING TIME)
COOKING TIME 35 MINUTES

3 cups (750ml) chicken stock
20g fresh galangal, sliced thickly
2 sticks fresh lemon grass,
cut into 5cm pieces
4 fresh kaffir lime leaves
2 teaspoons coarsely chopped
coriander root and stem
mixture
500g chicken thigh fillets,
sliced thinly
200g drained canned straw
mushrooms, rinsed
1 cup (250ml) coconut milk
1 tablespoon lime juice
1 tablespoon fish sauce
1 teaspoon grated palm sugar
1/4 cup loosely packed fresh
coriander leaves
2 fresh small red thai chillies,
deseeded, sliced thinly
2 fresh kaffir lime leaves,
shredded
1 stick fresh lemon grass,
sliced thinly

1 Combine stock, galangal, lemon grass pieces, whole lime leaves and coriander mixture in large saucepan; bring to a boil. Reduce heat; simmer, covered, 5 minutes. Remove from heat; stand 10 minutes. Strain stock through muslin into large heatproof bowl; discard solids.
2 Return stock to same cleaned pan. Add chicken and mushrooms; bring to a boil. Reduce heat; simmer, uncovered, about 5 minutes or until chicken is cooked through. Stir in coconut milk, juice, sauce and sugar; cook, stirring, until just heated through (do not allow to boil). Remove from heat; stir in coriander leaves, chilli, shredded lime leaves and lemon grass slices. Serve hot.

SERVES 4
PER SERVING 22.8G FAT; 1398KJ (334 CAL)

starters & soups

spicy sour prawn soup tom yum goong

PREPARATION TIME 20 MINUTES COOKING TIME 40 MINUTES

900g large uncooked king prawns
1 tablespoon peanut oil
1.5 litres (6 cups) water
2 tablespoons red curry paste (page 121)
1 tablespoon tamarind concentrate
2 tablespoons finely chopped fresh lemon grass
1 teaspoon ground turmeric
2 fresh small red thai chillies, seeded, chopped coarsely
1 tablespoon grated fresh ginger
6 fresh kaffir lime leaves, shredded finely
1 teaspoon grated palm sugar
100g shiitake mushrooms, halved
2 tablespoons fish sauce
2 tablespoons lime juice
1/4 cup loosely packed fresh vietnamese mint leaves
1/4 cup loosely packed fresh coriander leaves

1 Shell and devein prawns, leaving tails intact.
2 Heat oil in large saucepan; cook prawn shells and heads, stirring, about 5 minutes or until shells and heads are deep orange in colour.
3 Add 1 cup of the water and curry paste to pan; bring to a boil, stirring. Add remaining water; return to a boil. Reduce heat; simmer, uncovered, 20 minutes. Strain stock through muslin into large heat-proof bowl; discard solids.
4 Return stock to same cleaned pan. Add tamarind, lemon grass, turmeric, chilli, ginger, lime leaves and sugar; bring to a boil. Boil, stirring, 2 minutes. Reduce heat; add mushrooms; cook, stirring, 3 minutes. Add prawns; cook, stirring, until prawns are changed in colour. Remove from heat; stir in sauce and juice. Serve soup hot, topped with mint and coriander.

SERVES 4
PER SERVING 7.6G FAT; 781KJ (187 CAL)

pork and pickled garlic green curry
gaeng hang leh muu

PREPARATION TIME 20 MINUTES (PLUS MARINATING TIME)
COOKING TIME 20 MINUTES

1/4 cup (35g) coarsely chopped fresh ginger
3 cloves garlic, quartered
1 medium brown onion (150g), chopped coarsely
1 teaspoon ground turmeric
2 tablespoons green curry paste (page 121)
10 fresh kaffir lime leaves, torn
750g pork fillet, cut into 2cm cubes
1/4 cup (60ml) peanut oil
1 tablespoon tamarind concentrate
1 cup (250ml) boiling water
2 tablespoons fish sauce
2 bulbs pickled garlic (50g), drained, chopped coarsely
2 teaspoons grated palm sugar

1 Process or blend ginger, fresh garlic, onion, turmeric, curry paste and half of the lime leaves until mixture is almost smooth; combine in large bowl with pork. Toss to coat pork all over in marinade, cover; refrigerate at least 30 minutes.

2 Heat oil in large saucepan; cook pork mixture, stirring, until lightly browned all over.

3 Meanwhile, blend tamarind with the water in small jug; stir in fish sauce. Add tamarind mixture to pan; cook, uncovered, about 10 minutes or until pork is tender.

4 Add pickled garlic and sugar; simmer, stirring occasionally, about 5 minutes or until sauce thickens slightly.

5 Place curry in serving bowl; sprinkle with finely shredded remaining kaffir lime leaves.

SERVES 4
PER SERVING 21.2G FAT; 1650KJ (394 CAL)

curries

seafood and thai aubergine yellow curry
gaeng leuang taleh

PREPARATION TIME **30 MINUTES** COOKING TIME **30 MINUTES**

500g squid hoods
400g firm white fish fillets
8 medium uncooked prawns (200g)
8 medium black mussels (200g)
12 scallops (240g)
1 teaspoon shrimp paste
1 tablespoon peanut oil
2 tablespoons yellow curry paste
(page 120)
2 cloves garlic, crushed
2 teaspoons grated fresh ginger
1 medium brown onion (150g),
sliced thickly
1 stick fresh lemon grass, chopped finely
1 fresh long red thai chilli,
chopped coarsely
12 fresh thai aubergines (350g), quartered
1 cup (250ml) fish stock
400ml can coconut milk
3 fresh kaffir lime leaves, torn
1 tablespoon grated palm sugar
1/2 cup firmly packed fresh coriander leaves
2 tablespoons lime juice
2 fresh long red thai chillies, sliced thinly

1 Cut squid into 1.5cm slices and fish into 3cm pieces; shell and devein prawns, leaving tails intact. Scrub mussels; remove beards. Remove and discard any scallop roe.

2 Wrap shrimp paste in foil, place in heated wok or large saucepan; roast, tossing, until fragrant. Discard foil, return shrimp paste to same heated pan with oil and curry paste; stir over heat until blended.

3 Add garlic, ginger, onion, lemon grass and chopped chilli; cook, stirring, until onion softens. Add aubergine; cook, stirring, 2 minutes. Add stock, coconut milk, lime leaves and sugar; bring to a boil. Reduce heat; simmer, stirring occasionally, 10 minutes.

4 Add fish; cook, uncovered, 3 minutes. Add remaining seafood; cook, covered, about 5 minutes or until prawns change colour and mussels open (discard any that do not). Stir in coriander and juice.

5 Place curry in serving bowl; sprinkle with sliced chilli and coriander leaves, if desired.

SERVES **4**
PER SERVING 32.5G FAT; 2691KJ (643 CAL)

chicken panang curry
gaeng panaeng gai

2 x 400ml cans coconut milk
3 tablespoons panang curry paste (page 122)
2 tablespoons grated palm sugar
2 tablespoons fish sauce
2 fresh kaffir lime leaves, torn
2 tablespoons peanut oil
1kg chicken thigh fillets, quartered
100g snake beans, chopped coarsely
1/2 cup firmly packed fresh thai basil leaves
1/2 cup (75g) coarsely chopped roasted unsalted peanuts
2 fresh long red thai chillies, sliced thinly

1 Place coconut milk, paste, sugar, sauce and lime leaves in wok or large frying pan; bring to a boil. Reduce heat; simmer, stirring, about 15 minutes or until curry sauce mixture reduces by about a third.

2 Meanwhile, heat peanut oil in large frying pan; cook chicken, in batches, until browned lightly. Drain on absorbent paper.

3 Add beans, chicken and half of the basil leaves to curry sauce mixture; cook, uncovered, stirring occasionally, about 5 minutes or until beans are just tender and chicken is cooked through.

4 Place curry in serving bowl; sprinkle with peanuts, chilli and remaining basil.

SERVES 4
PER SERVING 82.1G FAT; 4347KJ (1038 CAL)

duck red curry
gaeng ped pet yang

PREPARATION TIME 15 MINUTES
COOKING TIME 15 MINUTES

$^1/_4$ cup (75g) red curry paste (page 121)
400ml can coconut milk
$^1/_2$ cup (125ml) chicken stock
2 fresh kaffir lime leaves, torn
1 tablespoon fish sauce
1 tablespoon lime juice
$^1/_3$ cup firmly packed fresh thai basil leaves
1 whole barbecued duck (1kg), cut into
12 pieces
565g can lychees, rinsed, drained
225g can bamboo shoots, rinsed, drained
3 fresh long red thai chillies, sliced thinly

1 Place curry paste in large saucepan; stir over heat until fragrant. Add coconut milk, stock, lime leaves, sauce and juice; bring to a boil. Reduce heat; simmer, stirring, 5 minutes.

2 Reserve about eight small whole basil leaves for garnish; add remaining basil leaves with duck, lychees and bamboo shoots to curry mixture. Cook, stirring occasionally, about 5 minutes or until heated through.

3 Place curry in serving bowl; sprinkle with sliced chilli and reserved thai basil leaves.

SERVES 4
PER SERVING 47.2G FAT; 2408KJ (575 CAL)

chicken green curry
gaeng keow wahn gai

PREPARATION TIME 20 MINUTES COOKING TIME 20 MINUTES

1/4 cup (75g) green curry paste
(page 121)
2 x 400ml cans coconut milk
2 fresh kaffir lime leaves, torn
1kg chicken thigh fillets
2 tablespoons peanut oil
2 tablespoons fish sauce
2 tablespoons lime juice
1 tablespoon grated palm sugar
150g pea aubergines, quartered
1 small courgette (150g), cut into
5cm pieces
1/3 cup loosely packed fresh thai
basil leaves
1/4 cup coarsely chopped fresh coriander
1 tablespoon fresh coriander leaves
1 fresh long green thai chilli, sliced thinly
2 green onions, sliced thinly

1 Place curry paste in large saucepan; stir over heat until fragrant. Add coconut milk and lime leaves; bring to a boil. Reduce heat; simmer, stirring, 5 minutes.
2 Meanwhile, quarter chicken pieces. Heat oil in large frying pan; cook chicken, in batches, until just browned. Drain on absorbent paper.
3 Add chicken to curry mixture with sauce, juice, sugar and aubergines; simmer, covered, about 5 minutes or until eggplants are tender and chicken is cooked through. Add courgette, basil and chopped coriander; cook, stirring, until courgette is just tender.
4 Place curry in serving bowl; sprinkle with coriander leaves, sliced chilli and onion.

SERVES 4
PER SERVING 72.4G FAT; 3826KJ (914 CAL)

pork jungle curry
gaeng pak prik muu

PREPARATION TIME 20 MINUTES   COOKING TIME 20 MINUTES

2 tablespoons peanut oil
1/4 cup (75g) red curry paste (page 121)
750g pork fillet, sliced thinly
1/3 cup firmly packed fresh thai basil leaves
40g pickled ka chai, sliced thinly
150g thai aubergines, chopped coarsely
1 medium carrot (150g), sliced thinly
100g snake beans, chopped coarsely
227g can bamboo shoots, rinsed, drained
2 x 5cm stems pickled green peppercorns (10g)
2 fresh kaffir lime leaves, torn
1 litre (4 cups) vegetable stock
4 fresh small red thai chillies, chopped coarsely

1 Place oil and curry paste in large saucepan; stir over heat until fragrant.
2 Add pork; cook, stirring, about 5 minutes or until browned all over.
3 Reserve about four large whole basil leaves for garnish. Add remaining basil leaves, ka chai, aubergine, carrot, beans, bamboo shoots, peppercorns, lime leaves and stock to pan; bring to a boil. Reduce heat; simmer, uncovered, about 10 minutes or until vegetables are tender. Stir in chilli.
4 Place curry in serving bowl; sprinkle with reserved thai basil leaves.

SERVES 4
PER SERVING 18.2G FAT; 1601KJ (382 CAL)

fish ball and aubergine red curry
gaeng luk chin pla

PREPARATION TIME 20 MINUTES   COOKING TIME 15 MINUTES

500g firm white fish fillets, chopped coarsely
1 clove garlic, quartered
1 tablespoon finely chopped coriander root and stem mixture
1 tablespoon soy sauce
1 tablespoon cornflour
2 teaspoons peanut oil
2 tablespoons red curry paste (page 121)
400ml can coconut milk
$^1/_2$ cup (60g) pea aubergines
2 teaspoons grated palm sugar
1 tablespoon lime juice
1 tablespoon fish sauce
2 spring onions, sliced thinly
$^1/_2$ cup (40g) bean sprouts
2 fresh long red thai chillies, sliced thinly
$^1/_4$ cup loosely packed fresh coriander leaves

1 Blend or process fish with garlic, coriander mixture, soy sauce and cornflour until mixture forms a smooth paste; roll heaped teaspoons of mixture into balls.

2 Place oil and curry paste in large saucepan; stir over heat until fragrant. Add coconut milk; bring to a boil, stirring, until blended. Add fish balls and aubergines, reduce heat; simmer, uncovered, about 5 minutes or until fish balls are cooked through. Stir in sugar, juice, fish sauce and onion; stir until sugar dissolves.

3 Place curry in serving bowl; sprinkle with sprouts, chilli and coriander leaves.

SERVES 4
PER SERVING 25.9G FAT; 1621KJ (387 CAL)

fish ball and green peppercorn red curry

PREPARATION TIME 30 MINUTES
COOKING TIME 15 MINUTES

750g firm white fish fillets, chopped coarsely
3 cloves garlic, quartered
2 tablespoons soy sauce
2 tablespoons cornflour
2 tablespoons finely chopped coriander root
and stem mixture
2cm piece fresh ginger (10g), grated
2 teaspoons peanut oil
$^1/_3$ cup (100g) red curry paste (page 121)
2 x 400g cans coconut milk
4 x 5cm stems pickled green peppercorns (20g),
rinsed, drained
2 teaspoons grated palm sugar
2 fresh kaffir lime leaves, shredded finely
2 teaspoons fish sauce
115g baby corn, halved lengthways
1 cup bean sprouts (80g)
1 fresh long red chilli, sliced thinly
$^1/_4$ cup loosely packed fresh coriander leaves

1   Blend or process fish, garlic, soy sauce, cornflour, coriander mixture and ginger until mixture forms a paste; roll level tablespoons of mixture into balls.
2   Cook oil and curry paste in large saucepan, stirring, until fragrant. Gradually stir in coconut milk; simmer, uncovered, 5 minutes. Add fish balls, peppercorn stems, sugar, lime leaves, fish sauce and corn; cook, uncovered, about 5 minutes or until fish balls are cooked through.
3   Serve curry sprinkled with sprouts, chilli and coriander leaves.

SERVES 4
PER SERVING 47.6G FAT; 2972KJ (711 CAL)

fish and potato yellow curry
gaeng leuang pla

PREPARATION TIME 20 MINUTES COOKING TIME 20 MINUTES

8 tiny new potatoes
(320g), halved
400ml can coconut milk
2 tablespoons yellow curry
paste (page 120)
$^1/_4$ cup (60ml) fish stock
2 tablespoons fish sauce
1 tablespoon lime juice
1 tablespoon grated palm sugar
800g firm white fish fillets,
cut into 3cm pieces
4 spring onions, sliced thinly
$^1/_3$ cup coarsely chopped
fresh coriander
1 fresh long red thai chilli,
deseeded, sliced thinly
1 tablespoon fresh coriander
leaves

1 Boil, steam or microwave potatoes until almost tender; drain.
2 Meanwhile, place half of the coconut milk in large saucepan; bring to a boil. Boil, stirring, until reduced by half and the oil has separated from the coconut milk. Add curry paste; cook, stirring, about 1 minute or until fragrant. Add remaining coconut milk, stock, sauce, juice and sugar; cook, stirring, until sugar dissolves.
3 Add fish and potato to pan; cook, stirring occasionally, about 3 minutes or until fish is cooked as desired. Stir in onion and chopped coriander.
4 Place curry in serving bowl; sprinkle with sliced chilli and coriander leaves.

SERVES 4
PER SERVING 24.2G FAT; 2004KJ (479 CAL)

duck jungle curry

PREPARATION TIME 40 MINUTES   COOKING TIME 2 HOURS

2kg duck
1/4 cup (60ml) peanut oil
1 medium brown onion (150g),
chopped coarsely
1 medium carrot (120g), chopped coarsely
2 cloves garlic, halved
4cm piece fresh ginger (20g), sliced thickly
1/2 teaspoon black peppercorns
2 litres (8 cups) cold water
5 fresh kaffir lime leaves, torn
1/4 cup (75g) red curry paste (page 121)
150g thai aubergines, halved
1 medium carrot (120g), sliced thinly
100g snake beans, cut into 4cm lengths
230g can bamboo shoots, rinsed, drained
2 x 5cm stems (10g) pickled green
peppercorns
1/2 cup firmly packed fresh thai basil leaves
4 fresh small red thai chillies,
chopped coarsely
2 tablespoons fish sauce

1 Discard neck then wash duck inside and out; pat dry with kitchen paper. Using sharp knife, separate drumstick and thigh sections from body; separate thighs from drumsticks. Remove and discard wings. Separate breast and backbone; cut breast from bone. You will have six pieces. Cut duck carcass into four pieces; discard any fat from carcass.
2 Heat 1 tablespoon of the oil in large saucepan; cook carcass pieces, stirring occasionally, about 5 minutes or until browned. Add onion, chopped carrot, garlic and ginger; cook, stirring, about 2 minutes or until onion softens. Add black peppercorns, the water and four of the lime leaves; simmer, uncovered, 1 hour 15 minutes, skimming fat from surface of mixture regularly.
3 Strain mixture through muslin-lined sieve into large heatproof jug. Reserve 3 cups of liquid; discard solids and remaining liquid.
4 Preheat oven to moderately hot (200°C/180°C fan-forced). Heat remaining oil in same cleaned pan; cook thighs, drumsticks and breasts, in batches, until browned. Remove skin from breasts and legs; slice skin thinly. Place sliced duck skin on oven tray; roast, uncovered, about 10 minutes or until crisp.
5 Discard excess oil from pan; reheat pan, cook curry paste, stirring, about 1 minute or until fragrant. Add aubergine, sliced carrot, beans, bamboo shoots, green peppercorns, half of the basil, remaining lime leaf and reserved liquid; simmer, uncovered, 5 minutes. Add duck pieces; simmer, uncovered, about 10 minutes or until vegetables are tender. Stir in chilli and sauce.
6 Place curry in serving bowls; sprinkle with remaining basil and crisped duck skin.

SERVES 4
PER SERVING 121G FAT; 5334KJ (1276 CAL)

beef massaman curry
gaeng masaman nuah

PREPARATION TIME 20 MINUTES COOKING TIME 2 HOURS

1kg beef skirt steak, cut into 3cm pieces
2 x 400ml cans coconut milk
1¹/2 cups (375ml) beef stock
5 cardamom pods, bruised
¹/4 teaspoon ground clove
2 star anise
1 tablespoon grated palm sugar
2 tablespoons fish sauce
1 tablespoon tamarind concentrate
2 tablespoons massaman curry paste
(page 122)
2 teaspoons tamarind concentrate, extra
¹/2 cup (125ml) beef stock, extra
8 small brown onions (300g), halved
1 medium sweet potato (400g),
chopped coarsely
¹/4 cup (35g) coarsely chopped
unsalted roasted peanuts
2 spring onions, sliced thinly

1 Place beef, half of the coconut milk, stock, cardamom, clove, star anise, sugar, sauce and tamarind in large saucepan; bring to a boil. Reduce heat; simmer, uncovered, about 1 hour 30 minutes or until beef is almost tender.

2 Strain beef over large bowl; reserve spicy beef sauce, discard cardamom and star anise.

3 Place curry paste in same cleaned pan; stir over heat until fragrant. Add remaining coconut milk, extra tamarind and stock; bring to a boil, stir for about 1 minute or until mixture is smooth. Add beef, brown onion, sweet potato and 1 cup of reserved spicy beef sauce; cook, uncovered, about 30 minutes or until vegetables and beef are tender.

4 Place curry in serving bowl; sprinkle with peanuts and spring onion before serving.

SERVES 4
PER SERVING 54.6G FAT; 3688KJ (881 CAL)

tamarind duck stir-fry
pad pet yang

PREPARATION TIME 20 MINUTES (PLUS STANDING TIME)
COOKING TIME 10 MINUTES

25g tamarind pulp
1/2 cup (125ml) boiling water
30g piece fresh ginger
1 tablespoon peanut oil
2 cloves garlic, crushed
2 fresh long red thai chillies, chopped finely
1 large whole barbecued duck (1kg), cut into 12 pieces
1 medium red pepper (200g), sliced thinly
1/4 cup (60ml) chicken stock
2 tablespoons oyster sauce
1 tablespoon fish sauce
2 tablespoons grated palm sugar
200g baby bok choy, chopped coarsely
100g mangetout, sliced thinly
8 spring onions, cut into 5cm lengths
1/3 cup firmly packed fresh coriander leaves

1 Soak tamarind pulp in the water for 30 minutes. Pour tamarind into a fine strainer over a small bowl; push as much pulp through the strainer as possible, scraping underside of strainer occasionally. Discard any tamarind solids left in strainer; reserve pulp liquid in bowl.
2 Slice peeled ginger thinly; stack slices, then slice again into very thin slivers.
3 Heat oil in wok; stir-fry ginger, garlic and chilli until fragrant. Add duck and pepper; stir-fry until pepper is tender and duck is heated through.
4 Add stock, sauces, sugar and reserved pulp liquid, bring to a boil; boil, 1 minute. Add bok choy; stir-fry until just wilted. Add mangetout and onion; stir-fry until both are just tender. Remove from heat; toss coriander leaves through stir-fry.

SERVES 4
PER SERVING 42.3G FAT; 2381KJ (569 CAL)

crisp hot and sweet beef with noodles
pad ped wan nuah

PREPARATION TIME 20 MINUTES (PLUS STANDING TIME)
COOKING TIME 1 HOUR 45 MINUTES

750g piece corned silverside
of beef
1kg fresh wide rice noodles
$1/4$ cup (60ml) peanut oil
3 cloves garlic, crushed
3 fresh small red thai chillies,
sliced thinly
4 large spring onions,
sliced thinly
2 tablespoons fish sauce
$1/4$ cup (65g) grated palm sugar
1 cup firmly packed fresh
coriander leaves

1 Place beef in large saucepan (see tip), cover with cold water; bring to a boil, uncovered. Reduce heat; simmer, covered, 1 hour 30 minutes. Remove from pan; drain beef on rack over tray for 15 minutes.
2 Meanwhile, place noodles in large heatproof bowl; cover with boiling water, separate with fork, drain.
3 Trim excess fat from beef; using two forks, shred beef finely. Heat oil in wok; stir-fry beef, in batches, until browned all over and crisp. Drain on absorbent paper.
4 Stir-fry garlic, chilli and onion in same wok until onion softens. Add sauce and sugar; stir-fry until sugar dissolves. Return beef to wok with noodles; stir-fry gently until heated through. Remove from heat; toss coriander leaves through stir-fry.

TIP Corned beef is best cooked in the vacuum packaging it is sold in; cook as above, discarding the packaging before draining the beef.
If cooked without the packaging, you can add some garlic, chillies, a few kaffir lime leaves and a stick of lemon grass to flavour the water, if you prefer.

SERVES 4
PER SERVING 20.6G FAT; 2589KJ (618 CAL)

ginger beef stir-fry   pad khing nuah

PREPARATION TIME **20 MINUTES**   COOKING TIME **10 MINUTES**

30g piece fresh ginger
2 tablespoons peanut oil
600g beef rump steak, sliced thinly
2 cloves garlic, crushed
120g snake beans, cut into 5cm lengths
8 spring onions, sliced thinly
2 teaspoons grated palm sugar
2 teaspoons oyster sauce
1 tablespoon fish sauce
1 tablespoon soy sauce
$^1/_2$ cup loosely packed fresh
thai basil leaves

1 Slice peeled ginger thinly; stack slices, then slice again into very thin slivers.
2 Heat half of the oil in wok; stir-fry beef, in batches, until browned all over.
3 Heat remaining oil in wok; stir-fry ginger and garlic until fragrant. Add beans; stir-fry until just tender.
4 Return beef to wok with onion, sugar and sauces; stir-fry until sugar dissolves and beef is cooked as desired. Remove from heat, toss basil leaves through stir-fry.

SERVES **4**
PER SERVING   19.8G FAT; 1536KJ (367 CAL)

stir-fried octopus with thai basil
pad pla muk horapa

PREPARATION TIME 20 MINUTES   COOKING TIME 10 MINUTES

1kg baby octopus
2 teaspoons peanut oil
2 teaspoons sesame oil
2 cloves garlic, crushed
2 fresh small red thai chillies, sliced thinly
2 large red peppers (500g), sliced thinly
6 spring onions, cut into 2cm lengths
1/4 cup firmly packed fresh thai basil leaves
1/4 cup (60ml) fish sauce
1/4 cup (65g) grated palm sugar
1 tablespoon kecap manis

1 Remove and discard the head and beak of each octopus; cut each octopus in half. Rinse under cold water; drain.

2 Heat peanut oil in wok; stir-fry octopus, in batches, until browned all over and tender. Cover to keep warm.

3 Heat sesame oil in same wok; stir-fry garlic, chilli and pepper until pepper is just tender. Return octopus to wok with remaining ingredients; stir-fry until basil leaves wilt and sugar dissolves.

SERVES 4
PER SERVING 6.4G FAT; 1048KJ (250 CAL)

pork with aubergine pad muu makeua

PREPARATION TIME 20 MINUTES COOKING TIME 25 MINUTES

3 fresh small red thai chillies, halved
6 cloves garlic, quartered
1 medium brown onion (150g), chopped coarsely
500g baby aubergines
2 tablespoons peanut oil
500g pork mince
1 tablespoon fish sauce
1 tablespoon soy sauce
1 tablespoon grated palm sugar
4 purple thai shallots, sliced thinly
150g snake beans, cut into 5cm lengths
1 cup loosely packed fresh thai basil leaves

1 Blend or process (or crush using mortar and pestle) chilli, garlic and onion until mixture forms a paste.

2 Quarter aubergines lengthways; slice each piece into 5cm lengths. Cook aubergines in large saucepan of boiling water until just tender; drain, pat dry with absorbent paper.

3 Heat oil in wok; stir-fry aubergines, in batches, until lightly browned. Drain on absorbent paper.

4 Stir-fry garlic paste in wok about 5 minutes or until lightly browned. Add pork; stir-fry until pork is changed in colour and cooked through. Add sauces and sugar; stir-fry until sugar dissolves. Add shallot and beans; stir-fry until beans are just tender. Return aubergines to wok; stir-fry, tossing gently until combined. Remove from heat; toss thai basil leaves through stir-fry.

SERVES 4
PER SERVING 18.9G FAT; 1387KJ (331 CAL)

prawns with garlic goong kratiem

PREPARATION TIME 20 MINUTES (PLUS MARINATING TIME)
COOKING TIME 5 MINUTES

1kg medium uncooked prawns
2 teaspoons coarsely chopped fresh
coriander root and stem mixture
2 teaspoons dried coriander seeds
1 teaspoon dried green peppercorns
4 cloves garlic, quartered
2 tablespoons peanut oil
1 cup (80g) bean sprouts
1 tablespoon finely chopped
fresh coriander
1 tablespoon packaged fried shallot
1 tablespoon packaged fried garlic
1 tablespoon fresh coriander leaves

1 Shell and devein prawns, leaving tails intact.
2 Crush coriander mixture, coriander seeds, peppercorns and garlic to a paste using mortar and pestle. Place paste in large bowl with prawns and half the oil; toss to coat prawns in marinade. Cover; refrigerate 3 hours or overnight.
3 Heat remaining oil in wok; stir-fry prawn mixture, in batches, until prawns are changed in colour. Remove from heat; toss bean sprouts and chopped coriander through stir-fry; serve sprinkled with fried shallot, fried garlic and coriander leaves.

SERVES 4
PER SERVING 11.2G FAT; 900KJ (215 CAL)

stir-fries

49

chicken and thai basil stir-fry
pad gai horapa

PREPARATION TIME 20 MINUTES COOKING TIME 15 MINUTES

2 tablespoons peanut oil
600g chicken breast fillets,
sliced thinly
2 cloves garlic, crushed
1 teaspoon grated fresh ginger
4 fresh small red thai chillies,
sliced thinly
4 kaffir lime leaves, shredded
1 medium brown onion
(150g), sliced thinly
100g mushrooms, quartered
1 large carrot (180g),
sliced thinly
1/4 cup (60ml) oyster sauce
1 tablespoon soy sauce
1 tablespoon fish sauce
1/3 cup (80ml) chicken stock
1 cup (80g) bean sprouts
3/4 cup loosely packed fresh
thai basil leaves

1 Heat half of the oil in wok; stir-fry chicken, in batches, until browned all over and cooked through.
2 Heat remaining oil in wok; stir-fry garlic, ginger, chilli, lime leaves and onion until onion softens and mixture is fragrant. Add mushroom and carrot; stir-fry until carrot is just tender. Return chicken to wok with sauces and stock; stir-fry until sauce thickens slightly. Remove from heat; toss bean sprouts and basil leaves through stir-fry.

SERVES 4
PER SERVING 18.2G FAT; 1449KJ (346 CAL)

deep-fried prawn balls   tod mun goong

PREPARATION TIME 25 MINUTES (PLUS STANDING TIME)
COOKING TIME 10 MINUTES

1kg uncooked large king prawns
5 spring onions, chopped finely
2 cloves garlic, crushed
4 fresh small red thai chillies,
deseeded, chopped finely
1 teaspoon grated fresh ginger
1 tablespoon cornflour
2 teaspoons fish sauce
1/4 cup coarsely chopped
fresh coriander
1/4 cup (25g) packaged
breadcrumbs
1/2 cup (35g) stale breadcrumbs
vegetable oil, for deep-frying
1/3 cup (80ml) sweet chilli sauce

1   Shell and devein prawns; cut in half. Blend or process prawn halves, pulsing, until chopped coarsely. Place in large bowl with onion, garlic, chilli, ginger, cornflour, sauce and coriander; mix well.
2   Using hands, roll rounded tablespoons of prawn mixture into balls. Roll prawn balls in combined breadcrumbs; place, in single layer, on plastic-wrap-lined tray. Cover, refrigerate 30 minutes.
3   Heat oil in wok or large saucepan; deep-fry prawn balls, in batches, until lightly browned and cooked through. Serve with sweet chilli sauce.

SERVES 4
PER SERVING 10.8G FAT; 1191KJ (284 CAL)

seafood

mixed seafood with crisp thai basil
pad taleh horapa

PREPARATION TIME **25 MINUTES** COOKING TIME **10 MINUTES**

250g squid hoods
250g firm white fish fillets
12 medium uncooked king prawns (600g)
250g baby octopus
2 tablespoons peanut oil
1 clove garlic, crushed
2 fresh small red thai chillies, sliced thinly
1 medium carrot (120g), halved, sliced thinly
1 medium red pepper (200g), sliced thinly
4 spring onions, sliced thinly
1 tablespoon fish sauce
1 teaspoon oyster sauce
1 tablespoon lime juice
1/4 cup (60ml) peanut oil, extra
1/3 cup loosely packed fresh thai basil leaves

1 Score squid in a diagonal pattern. Cut squid and fish into 3cm pieces; shell and devein prawns, leaving tails intact. Remove and discard the head and beak of each octopus; cut each octopus in half. Rinse under cold water; drain.

2 Heat half of the oil in wok or large saucepan; stir-fry seafood, in batches, until prawns are changed in colour, fish is cooked as desired, and squid and octopus are tender. Cover to keep warm.

3 Heat remaining oil in same wok; stir-fry garlic, chilli and carrot until carrot is just tender. Add pepper; stir-fry until pepper is just tender. Return seafood to wok with onion, sauces and juice; stir-fry, tossing gently, until hot.

4 Heat extra peanut oil in small frying pan until sizzling; fry basil leaves, in batches, until crisp but still green. Drain on absorbent paper. Top seafood with basil leaves.

SERVES 4
PER SERVING 16.3G FAT; 1455KJ (348 CAL)

seafood

55

mussels with basil and lemon grass hoy op

PREPARATION TIME 20 MINUTES COOKING TIME 10 MINUTES

1kg large mussels
(approximately 30)
1 tablespoon peanut oil
1 medium brown onion
(150g), chopped finely
2 cloves garlic, crushed
2 tablespoons thinly sliced
fresh lemon grass
1 fresh small red thai chilli,
chopped finely
1 cup (250ml) dry white wine
2 tablespoons lime juice
2 tablespoons fish sauce
1/2 cup loosely packed fresh
thai basil leaves
1/2 cup (125ml) coconut milk
1 fresh small red thai chilli,
seeded, sliced thinly
2 spring onions, sliced thinly

1 Scrub mussels under cold water; remove beards.
2 Heat oil in wok or large frying pan; stir-fry brown onion, garlic, lemon grass and chopped chilli until onion softens and mixture is fragrant.
3 Add wine, juice and sauce; bring to a boil. Add mussels; reduce heat, simmer, covered, about 5 minutes or until mussels open (discard any that do not).
4 Meanwhile, shred half of the basil finely. Add shredded basil and coconut milk to wok; stir-fry until heated through. Place mussel mixture in serving bowl; sprinkle with sliced chilli, spring onion and remaining basil.

SERVES 4
PER SERVING 12.2G FAT; 877KJ (209 CAL)

seafood

hot and sour fish steamed in banana leaves
hor neung mok pla

PREPARATION TIME 25 MINUTES (PLUS MARINATING TIME)
COOKING TIME 20 MINUTES

4 medium whole bream (1.8kg)
1 large banana leaf
4 fresh small red thai chillies, deseeded, sliced thinly
2 fresh kaffir lime leaves, shredded finely
2 spring onions, sliced thinly
1/4 cup loosely packed fresh coriander leaves
1/4 cup loosely packed fresh thai basil leaves
2 sticks fresh lemon grass
cotton string

LIME AND SWEET CHILLI DRESSING
1/4 cup (60ml) sweet chilli sauce
2 tablespoons fish sauce
2 tablespoons lime juice
2 tablespoons peanut oil
1 clove garlic, crushed
1 teaspoon grated fresh ginger

1 Make lime and sweet chilli dressing.
2 Score fish both sides through thickest part of flesh; place on large tray, drizzle with half of the lime and sweet chilli dressing. Cover; refrigerate 1 hour.
3 Meanwhile, trim banana leaf into four 30cm squares. Using tongs, dip one square at a time into large saucepan of boiling water; remove immediately. Rinse under cold water; pat dry with absorbent paper.
4 Place leaves on work surface. Combine chilli, lime leaves, onion, coriander and basil in medium bowl. Halve lemon grass sticks lengthways, then halve crossways; you will have eight pieces.
5 Place two pieces cut lemon grass on each leaf; place one fish on each. Top fish with equal amounts of the herb mixture then fold opposite corners of the leaf to enclose centre part of fish; secure each parcel with cotton string.
6 Place parcels, in single layer, in large bamboo steamer; steam, covered, in 2 batches, over wok or large frying pan of simmering water about 15 minutes or until fish is cooked through. Serve fish still in parcel, sprinkled with remaining dressing.

LIME AND SWEET CHILLI DRESSING Combine ingredients in screw-top jar; shake well.

SERVES 4
PER SERVING 22.1G FAT; 1708KJ (408 CAL)

TIP banana leaves can be ordered from greengrocers. Immersing them in hot water makes the leaves pliable and easy to use.
Foil can be used if banana leaves are unavailable.

seafood

salmon cutlets with green apple salad
yang pla yum poodza

PREPARATION TIME 20 MINUTES COOKING TIME 10 MINUTES
(PLUS COOLING TIME)

1/2 teaspoon sea salt
4 salmon cutlets (680g)
2 medium apples (300g),
sliced thinly
2 green onions, sliced thinly
1 medium red onion (170g),
sliced thinly
1 1/2 cups loosely packed
fresh mint leaves
3/4 cup loosely packed
fresh coriander leaves
1/2 cup (125ml) lemon juice
3/4 cup (110g) roasted
unsalted cashews

PALM SUGAR DRESSING
1/3 cup (65g) grated palm sugar
2 tablespoons fish sauce
2 teaspoons grated fresh ginger

1 Sprinkle salt evenly over fish. Cook fish on heated oiled griddle (or grill or barbecue) until browned both sides and cooked as desired.

2 Meanwhile, combine apple, onions, mint, coriander and juice in large bowl; pour over half of the palm sugar dressing, toss to combine. Divide fish among serving plates; top with salad, then cashews. Drizzle remaining dressing over fish.

PALM SUGAR DRESSING Combine ingredients in small saucepan; bring to a boil. Remove from heat; strain. Cool before using.

SERVES 4
PER SERVING 24G FAT; 2015KJ (481 CAL)

fish in spicy coconut cream pla tom kati

PREPARATION TIME 15 MINUTES   COOKING TIME 20 MINUTES

2 teaspoons peanut oil
2 cloves garlic, crushed
1 teaspoon grated fresh ginger
20g piece fresh turmeric, grated finely
2 fresh small red thai chillies, sliced thinly
1½ cups (375ml) fish stock
400ml can coconut cream
20g piece fresh galangal, halved
1 stick fresh lemon grass, cut into
2cm pieces
4 firm white fish fillets (800g)
2 tablespoons fish sauce
2 spring onions, sliced thinly

1 Heat oil in wok or large frying pan; cook garlic, ginger, turmeric and chilli, stirring, until fragrant. Add stock, coconut cream, galangal and lemon grass; bring to a boil. Add fish, reduce heat; simmer, covered, about 8 minutes or until fish is cooked as desired. Remove and discard galangal and lemon grass pieces.

2 Using slotted spoon, remove fish carefully from sauce; place in serving bowl, cover to keep warm. Bring sauce to a boil; boil 5 minutes. Remove from heat; stir in fish sauce and onion. Pour sauce over fish in bowl.

SERVES 4
PER SERVING 24.5G FAT; 1735KJ (414 CAL)

seafood

63

thai rices

Kin khao in Thai means both "rice" and "to eat": a meal without this staple food is simply unthinkable. Plain rice is served as the main part of every meal with various curries, soups and sauces presented in smaller bowls, their purpose being just to flavour the rice rather than being a main dish.

There are three main varieties grown in Thailand: jasmine white rice, sweet glutinous (sticky) rice and black (or purple) rice. Each of the rice cooking methods on the following pages makes enough rice for four servings.

glutinous

jasmine

black

glutinous rice

NOTE *Glutinous rice is a particular variety of rice that requires long soaking and steaming; other varieties of rice cannot be cooked by this method successfully.*

PREPARATION TIME 10 MINUTES (PLUS SOAKING TIME)
COOKING TIME 40 MINUTES

2 cups (400g) glutinous rice

1 Rinse rice in strainer or colander under cold water until water runs clear. Soak rice in large bowl of cold water overnight.
2 Drain rice. Line metal or bamboo steamer with muslin; place rice in steamer, cover tightly. Place steamer over large saucepan of boiling water, taking care that the bottom of the steamer does not touch the boiling water. Steam rice, tightly covered, about 40 minutes or until cooked as desired. Do not remove lid or stir rice during cooking time.

SERVES 4
PER SERVING 0.5G FAT; 1470KJ (351 CAL)

Thai glutinous rice (also known as 'sweet' or 'sticky' rice) is a uniquely flavoured rice that is eaten, formed into small balls, with the fingers and dipped into savoury dishes, to soak up their sauces. People in the north of Thailand eat glutinous rice as the main component of their diets. The grains are short, fat and chalky white in the centre, and cooked become soft and "sticky".

black rice

PREPARATION TIME 2 MINUTES COOKING TIME 20 MINUTES

2 cups (400g) black rice

1 Rinse rice in strainer under cold water until water runs clear.
2 Place rice in large saucepan of boiling water; boil, uncovered, stirring occasionally, about 20 minutes or until rice is cooked as desired. Drain; stand, covered, 10 minutes before serving.

SERVES 4
PER SERVING 0.6G FAT; 842KJ (201 CAL)

Black rice is also known as purple rice because, although a deep charcoal when raw, after cooking it turns a purplish-black colour. A medium-grain unmilled rice, with a white kernel under the black bran, it has a nutty, whole-grain flavour and is crunchy to the bite, similar to wild rice.

Thai jasmine rice is recognised around the world as having a particular aromatic quality that can almost be described as perfumed or floral. A long-grained white rice, it is some-times used in place of the more-expensive basmati rice in South-East Asia. Jasmine rice is rather moist in texture and clings together after cooking; adding salt during cooking is not recommended because it destroys the delicate flavour of the rice. No Thai meal is complete without a large bowl of hot jasmine rice at its epicentre.

jasmine rice

PREPARATION TIME 1 MINUTE (PLUS STANDING TIME)
COOKING TIME 12 MINUTES

2 cups (400g) jasmine rice
1 litre (4 cups) cold water

1 Combine rice and the water in large saucepan having a tight-fitting lid; bring to a boil, stirring occasionally.
2 Reduce heat as low as possible; cook rice, covered tightly, about 12 minutes or until all water is absorbed and rice is cooked as desired. Do not remove lid or stir rice during cooking time. Remove from heat; stand, covered, 10 minutes before serving.

SERVES 4
PER SERVING 0.5G FAT; 1470KJ (351 CAL)

*Chicken and thai basil fried rice
(see page 72)*

yellow coconut rice   khao kamin

PREPARATION TIME 5 MINUTES (PLUS STANDING TIME)
COOKING TIME 15 MINUTES

1³/4 cups (350g) long-grain
white rice
1¹/4 cups (310ml) water
400ml can coconut cream
¹/2 teaspoon salt
1 teaspoon sugar
¹/2 teaspoon ground turmeric
pinch saffron threads

1   Soak rice in large bowl of cold water for 30 minutes. Pour rice into strainer; rinse under cold water until water runs clear. Drain.
2   Place rice and remaining ingredients in large heavy-based saucepan; cover, bring to boil, stirring occasionally. Reduce heat; simmer, covered, about 15 minutes or until rice is tender. Remove from heat; stand, covered, 5 minutes.

SERVES 4
PER SERVING 21.1G FAT; 2167KJ (518 CAL)

chicken and thai basil fried rice
khao pad gai horapa

PREPARATION TIME 15 MINUTES COOKING TIME 10 MINUTES

1/4 cup (60ml) peanut oil
1 medium brown onion (150g),
chopped finely
3 cloves garlic, crushed
2 fresh long green thai chillies,
deseeded, chopped finely
1 tablespoon brown sugar
500g chicken breast fillets,
chopped coarsely
2 medium red peppers (400g),
sliced thinly
200g green beans, chopped coarsely
4 cups cooked jasmine rice
2 tablespoons fish sauce
2 tablespoons soy sauce
1/2 cup loosely packed fresh
thai basil leaves

1 Heat oil in wok; stir-fry onion, garlic and chilli until onion softens. Add sugar; stir-fry until dissolved. Add chicken; stir-fry until lightly browned. Add peppers and beans; stir-fry until vegetables are just tender and chicken is cooked through.

2 Add rice and sauces; stir-fry, tossing gently to combine. Remove from heat; add basil leaves, toss gently to combine.

SERVES 4
PER SERVING 21.7G FAT; 1922KJ (459 CAL)

crab fried rice in omelette
khai yud sai khao puu

PREPARATION TIME 15 MINUTES COOKING TIME 25 MINUTES

1/4 cup (60ml) peanut oil
4 spring onions, chopped finely
2 fresh small red thai chillies, chopped finely
1 tablespoon red curry paste (page 121)
2 cups cooked jasmine rice
250g fresh crab meat
2 tablespoons lime juice
2 tablespoons fish sauce
8 eggs
2 tablespoons water
1 lime, cut into wedges

1 Heat 1 tablespoon of the oil in wok; stir-fry onion and chopped chilli until onion softens. Add curry paste; stir-fry until mixture is fragrant.

2 Add rice; stir-fry until heated through. Remove from heat; place in large bowl. Add crab meat, juice and sauce; toss to combine.

3 Whisk eggs with the water in medium bowl. Heat about a quarter of the remaining oil in same cleaned wok; pour a quarter of the egg mixture into wok. Cook, tilting pan, over low heat until almost set. Spoon a quarter of the fried rice into centre of the omelette; using spatula, fold four sides of omelette over to enclose the filling.

4 Press omelette firmly with spatula; turn carefully to brown other side. Remove omelette from wok; cover to keep warm. Repeat process with remaining oil, egg mixture and fried rice. Place omelettes on serving plate; serve with lime.

SERVES 4
PER SERVING 26.3G FAT; 1599KJ (382 CAL)

chiang mai noodles   khao soi gai

PREPARATION TIME 20 MINUTES   COOKING TIME 20 MINUTES

vegetable oil, for deep-frying
500g fresh egg noodles
1 large brown onion (200g), sliced thinly
2 spring onions, sliced thinly
1/4 cup loosely packed fresh coriander leaves
1/4 cup (75g) red curry paste (page 121)
2 cloves garlic, crushed
1/4 teaspoon ground turmeric
2 cups (500ml) water
400ml can coconut milk
500g chicken breast fillets, sliced thinly
1/4 cup (60ml) fish sauce
1 tablespoon soy sauce
2 tablespoons grated palm sugar
2 teaspoons lime juice
2 tablespoons coarsely chopped fresh coriander
1 fresh long red thai chilli, deseeded, sliced thinly

1 Heat oil in wok; deep-fry about 100g of the noodles, in batches, until crisp. Drain on absorbent paper.

2 Using same heated oil, deep-fry brown onion, in batches, until lightly browned and crisp. Drain on absorbent paper. Combine fried noodles, fried onion, spring onion and coriander leaves in small bowl. Cool oil; remove from wok and reserve for another use.

3 Place remaining noodles in large heatproof bowl, cover with boiling water; use fork to separate noodles, drain.

4 Cook paste, garlic and turmeric in same cleaned wok, add the water and coconut milk; bring to a boil. Reduce heat; simmer, stirring, 2 minutes. Add chicken; cook, stirring, about 5 minutes or until chicken is cooked through. Add sauces, sugar and juice; cook, stirring, until sugar dissolves. Stir in chopped coriander.

5 Divide drained noodles among serving bowls; spoon chicken curry mixture into each bowl, then top with fried noodle mixture. Sprinkle chilli slices over each bowl.

SERVES 4
PER SERVING 33.5G FAT; 3358KJ (802 CAL)

sweet soy fried noodles   pad sieu

PREPARATION TIME 15 MINUTES COOKING TIME 15 MINUTES

1kg fresh wide rice noodles
2 teaspoons sesame oil
2 cloves garlic, crushed
2 fresh small red thai chillies, sliced thinly
600g chicken thigh fillets, chopped coarsely
250g baby bok choy, quartered lengthways
4 spring onions, sliced thinly
2 tablespoons kecap manis
1 tablespoon oyster sauce
1 tablespoon fish sauce
1 tablespoon grated palm sugar
$1/4$ cup coarsely chopped fresh coriander
1 tablespoon fried onion

1 Place noodles in large heatproof bowl; cover with boiling water, separate with fork, drain.
2 Heat oil in large wok; stir-fry garlic and chilli until fragrant. Add chicken; stir-fry until lightly browned. Add bok choy and spring onion; stir-fry until spring onion softens and chicken is cooked through.
3 Add noodles with kecap manis, sauces and sugar; stir-fry, tossing gently to combine. Remove from heat; add coriander, tossing gently to combine. Sprinkle with fried onion.

SERVES 4
PER SERVING 14.6G FAT; 2176KJ (520 CAL)

thai fried rice stick noodles   pad thai

PREPARATION TIME 20 MINUTES (PLUS STANDING TIME)
COOKING TIME 10 MINUTES

40g tamarind pulp
$1/2$ cup (125ml) boiling water
2 tablespoons grated palm sugar
$1/3$ cup (80ml) sweet chilli sauce
$1/3$ cup (80ml) fish sauce
375g rice stick noodles
12 medium uncooked prawns (500g)
2 cloves garlic, crushed
2 tablespoons finely chopped
preserved turnip
2 tablespoons dried shrimp
1 tablespoon grated fresh ginger
2 fresh small red thai chillies,
deseeded, chopped coarsely
1 tablespoon peanut oil
250g pork mince
3 eggs, beaten lightly
2 cups (160g) bean sprouts
4 spring onions, sliced thinly
$1/3$ cup coarsely chopped fresh coriander
$1/4$ cup (35g) coarsely chopped
roasted unsalted peanuts
1 lime, quartered

1 Soak tamarind pulp in the boiling water for 30 minutes. Pour tamarind into fine strainer over small bowl; push as much tamarind pulp through strainer as possible, scraping underside of strainer occasionally. Discard any tamarind solids left in strainer; reserve pulp liquid in bowl. Mix sugar and sauces into bowl with tamarind pulp; reserve.

2 Meanwhile, place noodles in large heatproof bowl; cover with boiling water, stand until noodles just soften; drain.

3 Shell and devein prawns, leaving tails intact.

4 Blend or process (or crush using mortar and pestle) garlic, turnip, shrimp, ginger and chilli until mixture forms a paste.

5 Heat oil in wok; stir-fry spice paste until fragrant. Add pork; stir-fry until just cooked through. Add prawns; stir-fry 1 minute. Add egg; stir-fry until egg just sets. Add noodles, tamarind mixture, sprouts and half of the onion; stir-fry, tossing gently until combined. Remove from heat; toss remaining spring onion, coriander and nuts through pad thai. Serve with lime wedges.

SERVES 4
PER SERVING 19.7G FAT; 2576KJ (615 CAL)

crisp fried noodles mee krob

PREPARATION TIME 35 MINUTES COOKING TIME 20 MINUTES

150g fresh silken firm tofu
vegetable oil, for deep-frying
125g rice vermicelli
2 tablespoons peanut oil
2 eggs, beaten lightly
1 tablespoon water
2 cloves garlic, crushed
2 fresh small red thai chillies,
chopped finely
1 fresh small green thai chilli,
chopped finely
2 tablespoons grated
palm sugar
2 tablespoons fish sauce
2 tablespoons tomato sauce
1 tablespoon rice wine vinegar
200g pork mince
200g small shelled cooked
prawns, chopped coarsely
6 spring onions, sliced thinly
1/4 cup firmly packed fresh
coriander leaves

1 Pat tofu all over with absorbent paper; cut into slices, then cut each slice into 1cm-wide matchsticks. Spread tofu on tray lined with absorbent paper; cover tofu with more absorbent paper, stand at least 10 minutes.

2 Meanwhile, heat vegetable oil in wok or large saucepan; deep-fry vermicelli quickly, in batches, until puffed. Drain on absorbent paper.

3 Using same heated oil, deep-fry drained tofu, in batches, until lightly browned. Drain on absorbent paper. Cool oil; remove from wok and reserve for another use.

4 Heat 2 teaspoons of the peanut oil in same cleaned wok; add half of the combined egg and water, swirl wok to make thin omelette. Cook, uncovered, until egg is just set. Remove from wok; roll omelette, cut into thin strips. Heat 2 more teaspoons of the peanut oil in same wok; repeat process with remaining egg mixture.

5 Combine garlic, chillies, sugar, sauces and vinegar in small bowl; pour half of the chilli mixture into small jug, reserve.

6 Combine pork in bowl with remaining half of the chilli mixture. Heat remaining peanut oil in same wok; stir-fry pork mixture about 5 minutes or until pork is cooked through. Add prawns; stir-fry 1 minute. Add tofu; stir-fry, tossing gently to combine.

7 Remove wok from heat; add reserved chilli mixture and half of the onion, toss to combine. Add vermicelli; toss gently to combine. Remove from heat; sprinkle with remaining onion, omelette strips and coriander leaves.

SERVES 4
PER SERVING 23.2G FAT; 2015KJ (481 CAL)

stir-fried aubergine tofu
pad makeua tao hu

PREPARATION TIME 15 MINUTES (PLUS STANDING TIME)
COOKING TIME 15 MINUTES

1 large aubergine (400g)
300g fresh firm silken tofu
1 medium brown onion (150g)
2 tablespoons peanut oil
1 clove garlic, crushed
2 fresh small red thai chillies, sliced thinly
1 tablespoon grated palm sugar
850g gai larn, chopped coarsely
2 tablespoons lime juice
$^1/_3$ cup (80ml) soy sauce
$^1/_3$ cup coarsely chopped fresh thai basil

1 Cut unpeeled aubergine in half lengthways; cut each half into thin slices. Place aubergine in colander, sprinkle with salt; let stand 30 minutes.
2 Meanwhile, pat tofu all over with absorbent paper; cut into 2cm squares. Spread tofu, in single layer, on absorbent-paper-lined tray; cover tofu with more absorbent paper, stand at least 10 minutes.
3 Cut onion in half, then cut each half into thin even-size wedges. Rinse aubergine under cold water; pat dry with absorbent paper.
4 Heat oil in wok; stir-fry onion, garlic and chilli until onion softens. Add sugar; stir-fry until dissolved. Add aubergine; stir-fry, 1 minute. Add gai larn; stir-fry until just wilted. Add tofu, juice and sauce; stir-fry, tossing gently until combined. Remove from heat; toss basil through stir-fry.

SERVES 4
PER SERVING 15.2G FAT; 1071KJ (256 CAL)

tofu and vegetable curry

PREPARATION TIME 25 MINUTES (PLUS STANDING TIME)
COOKING TIME 25 MINUTES

300g firm silken tofu
6 cloves garlic, quartered
3 fresh small red thai chillies, chopped coarsely
10cm stick (20g) fresh lemon grass, chopped coarsely
1.5cm piece fresh turmeric (20g), chopped coarsely
4cm piece fresh ginger (20g), chopped coarsely
1 medium brown onion (150g), chopped finely
1 tablespoon vegetable oil
400ml can coconut milk
1 cup (250ml) vegetable stock
2 fresh kaffir lime leaves
4 medium courgettes (480g), chopped coarsely
1 small cauliflower (1kg), cut into florets
1 tablespoon soy sauce
1 tablespoon lime juice
1/3 cup firmly packed fresh coriander, chopped coarsely
1/4 cup loosely packed fresh thai basil leaves

1 Press tofu between two chopping boards with a weight on top, raise one end; stand 10 minutes. Cut tofu into 2cm cubes; pat dry between layers of absorbent paper.

2 Blend or process garlic, chilli, lemon grass, turmeric, ginger, onion and oil until mixture forms a paste.

3 Cook garlic paste in large saucepan, stirring, 5 minutes. Add coconut milk, stock and lime leaves; simmer, uncovered, stirring occasionally, 10 minutes.

4 Add courgettes and cauliflower; simmer, uncovered, about 5 minutes or until vegetables are tender.

5 Discard lime leaves; stir in tofu, sauce, juice and coriander. Sprinkle with basil before serving.

SERVES 4

PER SERVING 31.7G FAT; 1843KJ (441 CAL)

vegetarian

pumpkin and bean curry

PREPARATION TIME 30 MINUTES
COOKING TIME 35 MINUTES

2 teaspoons ground cumin
2 teaspoons ground ginger
1 teaspoon ground coriander
1 tablespoon peanut oil
4 fresh long red chillies, sliced thinly
10cm stick (20g) fresh lemon grass,
sliced thinly
2 cloves garlic, crushed
4 fresh kaffir lime leaves, shredded finely
1 medium red onion (170g), sliced thinly
2 x 400ml cans coconut milk
1/3 cup (80ml) lime juice
1 tablespoon kecap manis
1 tablespoon grated palm sugar
1kg butternut squash, chopped coarsely
250g sugar snap peas, trimmed
200g snake beans, trimmed,
chopped coarsely
1 cup (140g) coarsely chopped roasted
unsalted peanuts
1/4 cup firmly packed fresh coriander leaves

1 Dry-fry spices in wok over medium heat,
stirring, about 1 minute or until fragrant. Add
oil, chilli, lemon grass, garlic, lime leaves and
onion; stir-fry until onion softens.
2 Add coconut milk, juice, kecap manis,
sugar and squash; simmer, uncovered, about
20 minutes or until squash softens. Stir in
peas and beans; cook, uncovered, about
5 minutes or until vegetables are just tender.
3 Serve curry sprinkled with nuts and fresh
coriander.

SERVES 4
PER SERVING 64.2G FAT); 3436KJ (822 CAL)

larb tofu larb tao hu

PREPARATION TIME 20 MINUTES (PLUS STANDING TIME)
COOKING TIME 10 MINUTES

900g fresh firm silken tofu
peanut oil, for deep-frying
1 medium red onion (170g),
chopped finely
$^1/_2$ cup coarsely chopped
fresh coriander
1 tablespoon finely chopped
fresh lemon grass
2 fresh small red thai chillies,
chopped finely
2 tablespoons lemon juice
1 teaspoon grated palm sugar
1 tablespoon soy sauce
$^1/_2$ teaspoon sambal oelek
8 small chinese cabbage
leaves (360g)

1 Pat tofu with absorbent paper; chop finely. Spread tofu, in single layer, on absorbent-paper-lined tray; cover tofu with more absorbent paper, stand at least 20 minutes.

2 Heat oil in wok or large saucepan; deep-fry tofu, in batches, until lightly browned. Drain on absorbent paper.

3 Combine tofu in large bowl with onion, coriander, lemon grass and chilli. Combine juice, sugar, sauce and sambal in small jug; stir until sugar dissolves. Pour dressing over tofu mixture; toss to combine. Serve spooned into individual whole cabbage leaves.

SERVES 4
PER SERVING 27.7G FAT; 1641KJ (392 CAL)

vegetarian pad thai

PREPARATION TIME 20 MINUTES (PLUS STANDING TIME)
COOKING TIME 10 MINUTES

200g rice stick noodles
2 cloves garlic, quartered
2 tablespoons finely chopped preserved turnip
2 fresh small red thai chillies, seeded, chopped coarsely
1/4 cup (60ml) peanut oil
2 eggs, beaten lightly
1 cup (90g) fried onion
125g fried tofu, cut into small pieces
1/4 cup (35g) coarsely chopped roasted unsalted peanuts
3 cups (240g) bean sprouts
6 spring onions, sliced thinly
2 tablespoons soy sauce
1 tablespoon lime juice
2 tablespoons coarsely chopped fresh coriander

1 Place noodles in large heatproof bowl; cover with boiling water, stand until noodles just soften, drain.
2 Meanwhile, using mortar and pestle, crush garlic, turnip and chilli until mixture forms a paste.
3 Heat 2 teaspoons of the oil in wok; pour in egg, swirl wok to make thin omelette. Cook, uncovered, until egg is just set. Remove from wok; roll omelette, cut into thin strips.
4 Heat remaining oil in wok; stir-fry garlic paste and fried onion until fragrant. Add tofu; stir-fry 1 minute. Add half of the nuts, half of the sprouts and half of the spring onion; stir-fry until sprouts are just wilted. Add noodles, sauce and juice; stir-fry, tossing gently until combined. Remove from heat; toss remaining nuts, sprouts and spring onion with omelette strips and coriander through pad thai. Serve with lime wedges, if desired.

SERVES 4

PER SERVING 27G FAT; 1813KJ (433 CAL)

stir-fried cauliflower, choy sum and snake beans   pad pak ruam

PREPARATION TIME 20 MINUTES   COOKING TIME 10 MINUTES

1 tablespoon peanut oil
2 cloves garlic, crushed
1 teaspoon ground turmeric
1 teaspoon finely chopped
coriander root and stem mixture
4 green onions, sliced thinly
500g cauliflower florets
1/4 cup (60ml) water
200g snake beans, cut into
5cm pieces
200g choy sum, chopped coarsely
1 tablespoon lime juice
1 tablespoon soy sauce
1 tablespoon coarsely chopped
fresh coriander

1 Heat oil in wok; cook garlic, turmeric, coriander mixture and onion; stir-fry until onion just softens. Remove from wok; keep warm.
2 Stir-fry cauliflower with the water in same wok until cauliflower is almost tender. Add beans and choy sum; stir-fry until vegetables are just tender.
3 Add juice, sauce, chopped coriander and onion mixture; stir-fry until heated through.

SERVES 4
PER SERVING 5.4G FAT; 385KJ (92 CAL)

vegetarian

91

mixed vegetables in coconut milk
pak tom kati

PREPARATION TIME 25 MINUTES COOKING TIME 15 MINUTES

6 cloves garlic, quartered
3 fresh small red thai chillies, chopped coarsely
2 tablespoons coarsely chopped fresh lemon grass
1 tablespoon coarsely chopped pickled galangal
20g piece fresh ginger, chopped coarsely
20g piece fresh turmeric, chopped coarsely
2 cups (500ml) coconut milk
2 whole kaffir lime leaves
4 medium courgettes (480g), chopped coarsely
6 yellow patty-pan squash (240g), chopped coarsely
200g cauliflower florets
100g baby corn, halved lengthways
2 tablespoons soy sauce
2 tablespoons lime juice
1/3 cup coarsely chopped fresh thai basil
2 kaffir lime leaves, shredded finely

1 Blend or process (or crush using mortar and pestle) garlic, chilli, lemon grass, galangal, ginger and turmeric until mixture forms a paste.

2 Place half of the coconut milk in wok or large saucepan; bring to a boil. Add garlic paste; whisk over high heat until smooth. Reduce heat, add remaining coconut milk and whole lime leaves; simmer, stirring, until coconut milk mixture thickens slightly.

3 Add courgettes, squash, cauliflower and corn; bring to a boil. Reduce heat; simmer, uncovered, about 5 minutes or until vegetables are just tender. Remove from heat; remove and discard whole lime leaves. Stir sauce, juice and basil into vegetable mixture; serve topped with shredded lime leaves.

SERVES 4
PER SERVING 26.9G FAT; 1406KJ (336 CAL)

pumpkin, basil and chilli stir-fry
pad pet fak tong

PREPARATION TIME 10 MINUTES   COOKING TIME 15 MINUTES

$^{1}/_{3}$ cup (80ml) peanut oil
1 large brown onion (200g), sliced thinly
2 cloves garlic, sliced thinly
4 fresh small red thai chillies, sliced thinly
1kg pumpkin, chopped coarsely
250g sugar snap peas
1 teaspoon grated palm sugar
$^{1}/_{4}$ cup (60ml) vegetable stock (page 117)
2 tablespoons soy sauce
$^{3}/_{4}$ cup loosely packed opal basil leaves
4 spring onions, sliced thinly
$^{1}/_{2}$ cup (75g) roasted unsalted peanuts

1 Heat oil in wok; cook brown onion, in batches, until browned and crisp. Drain on absorbent paper.
2 Stir-fry garlic and chilli in wok until fragrant. Add pumpkin; stir-fry until browned all over and just tender. Add peas, sugar, stock and sauce; stir-fry until sauce thickens slightly.
3 Remove from heat; toss basil, spring onion and nuts through stir-fry until well combined. Serve topped with fried onion.

SERVES 4
PER SERVING 20.7G FAT; 1436KJ (343 CAL)

vegetarian

95

pomelo salad   yum som-o

PREPARATION TIME 30 MINUTES

1 small red onion (100g)
4 large pomelos (4kg)
2 spring onions, sliced thinly
2 fresh small red thai chillies, sliced thinly
$^1/_4$ cup coarsely chopped fresh coriander
$^1/_2$ cup (70g) coarsely chopped roasted unsalted peanuts
2 cloves garlic, crushed
1 tablespoon grated palm sugar
$^1/_4$ cup (60ml) lime juice
1 tablespoon soy sauce

1 Halve red onion; cut each half into paper-thin wedges.
2 Peel and carefully segment pomelos; discard membranes. Combine segments in large bowl with onions, chilli, coriander and nuts.
3 Combine remaining ingredients in small jug; stir until sugar dissolves. Pour dressing over pomelo mixture; toss gently to combine.

SERVES 4
PER SERVING 10.6G FAT; 1311KJ (313 CAL)

vegetarian

96

salads

char-grilled beef salad   yum nuah

PREPARATION TIME 15 MINUTES (PLUS MARINATING TIME)
COOKING TIME 10 MINUTES

500g beef rump steak
$1/4$ cup (60ml) fish sauce
$1/4$ cup (60ml) lime juice
3 cucumbers (390g), deseeded, sliced thinly
4 fresh small red thai chillies, sliced thinly
8 spring onions, sliced thinly
250g cherry tomatoes, quartered
1 cup loosely packed vietnamese mint leaves
1 cup loosely packed coriander leaves
1 tablespoon grated palm sugar
2 teaspoons soy sauce
1 clove garlic, crushed

1 Combine beef with 2 tablespoons of the fish sauce and 1 tablespoon of the juice in large bowl; cover, refrigerate 3 hours or overnight.
2 Drain beef; discard marinade. Cook beef on heated oiled griddle (or grill or barbecue) until browned both sides and cooked as desired. Cover, stand 5 minutes; slice thinly.
3 Meanwhile, combine cucumber, chilli, onion, tomato and herbs in large bowl. Combine remaining juice and fish sauce with sugar, soy sauce and garlic in screw-top jar; shake well.
4 Add beef and dressing to salad; toss gently to combine.

SERVES 4
PER SERVING 8.7G FAT; 1008KJ (241 CAL)

crab salad yum pla-puu

PREPARATION TIME 15 MINUTES

500g fresh crab meat
250g chinese cabbage, chopped finely
1 cucumber (130g), deseeded,
chopped coarsely
1 medium red onion (170g), halved,
sliced thinly
6 spring onions, cut into 4cm lengths
1 cup loosely packed fresh
thai mint leaves

DRESSING

2 cloves garlic, crushed
2 tablespoons lime juice
2 tablespoons fish sauce
1 tablespoon brown sugar
2 fresh small red thai chillies,
chopped finely

1 Drain crab in strainer; remove any shell and if necessary shred the meat to desired texture.
2 Combine crab in large bowl with cabbage, cucumber, onions and mint; pour in dressing, toss to combine.

DRESSING Combine all ingredients in screw-top jar; shake well.

SERVES 4
PER SERVING 1G FAT; 529KJ (126 CAL)

salads

101

crisp fish salad with chilli lime dressing
yum pla foo

PREPARATION TIME 20 MINUTES COOKING TIME 30 MINUTES

250g firm white fish fillets
vegetable oil, for deep-frying
1 medium red onion (170g), sliced thinly
6 spring onions, sliced thinly
2 cucumbers (260g), deseeded, sliced thinly
1 cup firmly packed thai mint leaves
1 cup firmly packed coriander leaves
2 tablespoons coarsely chopped roasted unsalted peanuts
2 teaspoons finely grated lime rind

CHILLI LIME DRESSING
4 fresh small green thai chillies, deseeded, chopped finely
2 tablespoons fish sauce
1/3 cup (80ml) lime juice
1 tablespoon brown sugar

1 Preheat oven to moderate. Place fish on wire rack over oven tray; roast, uncovered, 20 minutes. When cool enough to handle, cut fish into pieces, then blend or process, pulsing, until mixture resembles coarse breadcrumbs.

2 Heat oil in wok or deep frying pan; deep-fry processed fish, in batches, until lightly browned and crisp. Drain on absorbent paper.

3 Combine onions, cucumber and herbs in large bowl; add chilli lime dressing, toss to combine. Sprinkle salad with crisp fish, nuts and lime rind; serve immediately.

CHILLI LIME DRESSING Combine ingredients in screw-top jar; shake well.

SERVES 4
PER SERVING 7.1G FAT; 711KJ (170 CAL)

salad of asian greens

PREPARATION TIME 20 MINUTES

1 small chinese cabbage (700g), sliced thinly
1 red oak leaf lettuce (380g), torn
100g mizuna
100g mangetout sprouts, trimmed
100g mangetout, trimmed, sliced thinly
$^{1}/_{2}$ small white radish (200g), sliced thinly
4 spring onions, sliced thinly

SESAME AND GINGER DRESSING
$^{1}/_{3}$ cup (80ml) low salt soy sauce
2 tablespoons white vinegar
2 teaspoons sesame oil
1cm piece fresh ginger (5g), grated
1 clove garlic, crushed

1 Place ingredients for sesame and ginger dressing in screw-top jar; shake well.
2 Place salad ingredients in large bowl with dressing; toss gently to combine.

SERVES 10
PER SERVING 1.4G FAT; 192KJ (46 CAL)

cold prawn salad yum goong wun sen

PREPARATION TIME 20 MINUTES (PLUS STANDING TIME)

200g bean thread noodles
1 clove garlic, crushed
2 tablespoons fish sauce
1 tablespoon lime juice
2 teaspoons peanut oil
1/4 cup (35g) coarsely chopped roasted unsalted peanuts
2 green onions, sliced thinly
1/4 cup coarsely chopped fresh coriander
2 fresh small red thai chillies, deseeded, sliced thinly
1kg large cooked king prawns, peeled, deveined

1 Place noodles in large heatproof bowl; cover with boiling water. Stand until just tender; drain. Using kitchen scissors, cut noodles into random lengths.

2 Whisk garlic, sauce, juice and oil in large bowl to combine.

3 Add noodles to bowl with nuts, onion, coriander, chilli and prawns; toss gently to combine.

SERVES 4
PER SERVING 7.8G FAT; 1353KJ (323 CAL)

pork and lychee salad   yum muu lynchee

PREPARATION TIME 20 MINUTES (PLUS STANDING TIME)
COOKING TIME 10 MINUTES

1 tablespoon peanut oil
300g pork fillet
565g can lychees, rinsed, drained, halved
1 medium red pepper (200g), sliced thinly
1 stick fresh lemon grass, sliced thinly
2 fresh kaffir lime leaves, shredded finely
100g watercress
2 tablespoons coarsely chopped fresh vietnamese mint
2 tablespoons drained thinly sliced pickled ginger
2 tablespoons fried shallot

PICKLED GARLIC DRESSING
1 tablespoon drained finely chopped pickled garlic
2 fresh small red thai chillies, deseeded, sliced thinly
1 tablespoon rice vinegar
1 tablespoon lime juice
1 tablespoon fish sauce
1 tablespoon palm sugar

1 Heat oil in wok; cook pork, turning, until browned all over and cooked as desired. Cover, stand 10 minutes; slice thinly. Place pork in medium bowl with pickled garlic dressing; toss to coat pork all over. Stand 10 minutes.

2 Meanwhile, combine lychees, pepper, lemon grass, lime leaves, watercress and mint in large bowl.

3 Add pork mixture to lychee mixture; toss gently to combine. Serve sprinkled with pickled ginger and fried shallot.

PICKLED GARLIC DRESSING Combine all ingredients in screw-top jar; shake well.

SERVES 4
PER SERVING 7.4G FAT; 920KJ (220 CAL)

spicy chicken salad larb gai

PREPARATION TIME 25 MINUTES   COOKING TIME 20 MINUTES

2 tablespoons long-grain white rice
1 tablespoon peanut oil
1 tablespoon finely chopped fresh lemon grass
2 fresh small red thai chillies, deseeded, chopped finely
2 cloves garlic, crushed
1 tablespoon finely chopped fresh galangal
750g chicken mince
1 cucumber (130g), deseeded, sliced thinly
1 small red onion (100g), sliced thinly
100g bean sprouts
1/2 cup loosely packed fresh thai basil leaves
1 cup loosely packed fresh coriander leaves
4 large iceberg lettuce leaves

DRESSING
1/3 cup (80ml) lime juice
2 tablespoons fish sauce
2 tablespoons kecap manis
2 tablespoons peanut oil
2 teaspoons grated palm sugar
1/2 teaspoon sambal oelek

1 Heat dry wok; stir-fry rice until lightly browned. Blend or process (or crush using mortar and pestle) rice until it resembles fine breadcrumbs.

2 Heat oil in same wok; stir-fry lemon grass, chilli, garlic and galangal until fragrant. Remove from wok. Stir-fry chicken, in batches, until changed in colour and cooked through.

3 Return chicken and lemon grass mixture to wok with about 1/3 of the dressing; stir-fry about 5 minutes or until mixture thickens slightly.

4 Place remaining dressing in large bowl with chicken, cucumber, onion, sprouts and herbs; toss gently to combine. Place lettuce leaves on serving plates; divide larb salad among leaves, sprinkle with ground rice.

DRESSING Combine all ingredients in screw-top jar; shake well.

SERVES 4
PER SERVING 29.7G FAT; 1997KJ (477 CAL)

green papaya salad som tum

PREPARATION TIME 25 MINUTES COOKING TIME 3 MINUTES

100g snake beans
850g green papaya
250g cherry tomatoes, quartered
3 fresh small green thai chillies, deseeded, chopped finely
2 tablespoons finely chopped dried shrimp
1/4 cup (60ml) lime juice
1 tablespoon fish sauce
1 tablespoon grated palm sugar
2 cloves garlic, crushed
1/4 cup coarsely chopped fresh coriander
2 cups (120g) finely shredded iceberg lettuce
1/3 cup (50g) coarsely chopped roasted unsalted peanuts

1 Cut beans in 5cm pieces; cut pieces in half lengthways. Boil, steam or microwave beans until just tender; drain. Rinse immediately under cold water; drain.
2 Meanwhile, peel papaya. Quarter lengthways, remove seeds; grate papaya coarsely.
3 Place papaya and beans in large bowl with tomato, chilli and shrimp. Add combined juice, sauce, sugar, garlic and half of the coriander; toss gently to combine.
4 Place lettuce on serving plates; spoon papaya salad over lettuce, sprinkle with nuts and remaining coriander.

SERVES 4
PER SERVING 7G FAT; 677KJ (162 CAL)

drinks

thai bloody mary

PREPARATION TIME **5 MINUTES**

Crush 1 teaspoon grated palm sugar, 2 finely shredded fresh kaffir lime leaves, 1 fresh small red thai chilli and 20ml lime juice in cocktail shaker. Add 60ml vodka, 1 cup ice cubes and dash fish sauce; shake vigorously. Pour into 340ml highball glass. Top with 150ml vegetable juice; stir to combine. Garnish with lime wedge.

papaya, strawberry and orange frappé

PREPARATION TIME **10 MINUTES**

Use the red-fleshed Hawaiian or Fijian variety instead of the yellow-fleshed papaya in this recipe. Blend or process 1 large coarsely chopped papaya (1.5kg), 250g strawberries and 180ml chilled orange juice until smooth.

MAKES **1 LITRE**

watermelon refresher

PREPARATION TIME 10 MINUTES

Buy a 1.5kg piece of watermelon for this recipe. Blend or process 900g coarsely chopped seedless watermelon, 125ml chilled orange juice and 40ml lime juice until smooth. Garnish with lime slices.

MAKES 1 LITRE

virgin sea breeze

PREPARATION TIME 5 MINUTES

Place 500ml chilled cranberry juice, 500ml chilled ruby red grapefruit juice and 40ml lime juice in large jug; stir to combine.

MAKES 1 LITRE

drinks

lemon grass spritzer

PREPARATION TIME 10 MINUTES
(PLUS REFRIGERATION TIME)
COOKING TIME 5 MINUTES

Place $^1/_3$ cup (90g) grated palm sugar and 125ml water in small saucepan; stir, over low heat, until sugar dissolves. Remove from heat; stir in 2 tablespoons coarsely chopped fresh lemon grass. Cover and refrigerate until chilled. Combine strained sugar mixture with 125ml lime juice, 750ml chilled sparkling mineral water and 1 cup ice cubes in large jug.

MAKES 1 LITRE

ginger beer iced tea

PREPARATION TIME 5 MINUTES

Combine 15ml vodka, 15ml white rum, 15ml white tequila, 15ml gin, 10ml Cointreau, 15ml lime juice, 15ml sugar syrup* and $^1/_2$ cup ice cubes in cocktail shaker; shake vigorously. Pour into 250ml highball glass. Top with 80ml ginger beer; garnish with lime slice.

*SUGAR SYRUP Stir 1 cup (220g) caster sugar with 1 cup (250ml) water in small saucepan, over low heat, until sugar dissolves; bring to a boil. Reduce heat; simmer, uncovered, without stirring, 5 minutes. Remove from heat; cool to room temperature.

drinks

114

apple and grapefruit juice with cinnamon sticks

PREPARATION TIME 5 MINUTES
(PLUS REFRIGERATION TIME)
COOKING TIME 5 MINUTES

Combine 1 litre (4 cups) apple juice and 4 cinnamon sticks, halved lengthways, in medium saucepan. Bring to a boil. Remove from heat; cool to room temperature. Transfer to large jug, cover; refrigerate 3 hours or overnight. Add 1 litre (4 cups) grapefruit juice to apple juice mixture; stir to combine. Serve juice with cinnamon stick.

MAKES 2 LITRES

chai tea

PREPARATION TIME 10 MINUTES
(PLUS REFRIGERATION TIME)

Combine 2 teaspoons honey, 1 teaspoon ground cardamom, $1/2$ teaspoon ground cinnamon, $1/2$ teaspoon ground cloves, $1/2$ teaspoon ground ginger and 395g can sweetened condensed milk in small bowl. Cover; refrigerate overnight. Place an english breakfast tea bag in each of 8 cups or tea glasses. Add boiling water to the cups; stand 3 minutes. Discard tea bags; stir 1 teaspoon of the spiced milk mixture into each cup.

SERVES 8

drinks

curry pastes

Much of Thai food has its roots in cuisines native to the many traders and immigrants who arrived in Thailand in the distant past, and one of these influences came from southern India. Indian curries evolved from being just condiments to add to the main meal of rice, to the many different robust dishes we are familiar with today. Since rice has always been an indispensable part of the Thai table, the concept of various sauces created intentionally to add different savoury flavours to rice was the original basis of many Thai curry pastes. And the coconut milk used in southern Indian curries to season, thicken and serve as a chilli-tempering foil happily found its niche in the Thai kitchen.

tips & techniques

Thai curries are made from far more than just a blend of dried spices or the ubiquitous canned yellow powder with which we are all familiar. A Thai curry paste is an amalgam of fresh herbs, aromatic spices, dried and fresh chillies, fruits, seafood, stems, roots and shoots, smashed or ground together in various proportions to make complex-tasting, intensely flavoured pastes.

Traditionally, curry paste is made with a mortar and pestle but, for ease and speed, we made our paste recipes in a blender or food processor. If your machine cannot break down the ingredients' fibrous content into a smooth paste, we suggest that you first pulverise them in a blender or processor until they become pulpy, then transfer the mixture to a mortar and pestle for a final grinding. However you decide to make a curry paste, you should aim for a result that is thick but not lumpy, to guarantee homogeneity of flavour.

It's a good idea to have all the ingredients ready for use before you start to process the paste

curry pastes

There are many bottled and canned curry pastes available at Asian food stores and your local supermarket, some imported from Thailand while others are made locally, and, if you don't have time to make one, these commercial pastes will do the job. However, if it's authenticity you're after, only a homemade curry paste gives you that complex but harmonious blend of the four distinct tastes inherent to the food of Thailand – sweet, salty, spicy and sour (and, to a lesser degree, a fifth, bitter).

Since they keep well, curry pastes can be prepared in quantity so you have plenty at hand for future use. Each recipe on the following pages makes a cup of curry paste, more than is required for any one recipe, so you'll have them ready and waiting whenever you next want to cook Thai food.

Use what you need at the time, then place the remaining paste in a glass jar, cover it tightly and refrigerate it for up to a week. A better idea is to make the paste, use what you want for that occasion, then freeze the rest. Place tablespoons of curry paste in the compartments of an ice-cube tray; wrap the tray tightly in plastic wrap and put it in your freezer until the paste solidifies. Remove the blocks of curry paste, then re-wrap them individually and return to the freezer until required. This way you'll never need to thaw more than you need at any given time. You can store curry pastes this way for up to three months with no discernible difference in flavour.

We've given recipes for a handful of the most popular curry pastes but, once you've experimented with these, don't feel locked into our formulas forever. Add to, alter or delete ingredients according to your taste preferences. Like garlic? Double what we suggest. Afraid of too much chilli? Gradually decrease the amounts suggested.

Curry pastes are, as the name implies, an essential ingredient in the making of a Thai curry, but they can be used in any number of other dishes, from stir-fries and salads to soups and marinades. Every dish you add them to, no matter how quickly it's prepared, will taste as though it's been slowly simmered for hours, such is its depth and complexity of flavour.

Dry-fry the various spices in a small frying pan in order to bring out their dormant flavours

To achieve a smooth curry paste, finish blending the ingredients with a mortar and pestle

With the exception of the massaman paste (which, like its Indian forebears, takes about 15 minutes in a hot oven to dry-roast the spices), these recipes only take a little cooking time, and will keep, covered tightly, in the refrigerator for up to a week. See our tips on the previous page for freezing curry pastes. Each recipe makes 1 cup (300g) curry paste.

yellow curry paste
gaeng leuang

PREPARATION TIME **20 MINUTES** COOKING TIME **3 MINUTES**

1 teaspoon ground coriander
1 teaspoon ground cumin
$1/2$ teaspoon ground cinnamon
1 teaspoon finely chopped fresh turmeric
5 fresh long yellow chillies, chopped coarsely
2 large cloves garlic, quartered
1 medium (150g) brown onion, chopped coarsely
2 tablespoons finely chopped fresh lemon grass
2 teaspoons finely chopped fresh galangal
1 tablespoon coarsely chopped fresh coriander root and stem mixture
1 teaspoon shrimp paste
1 tablespoon peanut oil

1 Stir ground coriander, cumin and cinnamon over medium heat in small dry-heated frying pan until fragrant.
2 Blend or process roasted spices with remaining ingredients, except for the oil, until mixture forms a paste, pausing to scrape down sides of machine occasionally during blending.
3 Add oil to paste mixture; continue to blend in machine or using mortar and pestle until smooth.

Top: fish and potato yellow curry; centre: chicken green curry; bottom: duck red curry

green curry paste
gaeng keow wahn

PREPARATION TIME 20 MINUTES COOKING TIME 3 MINUTES

2 teaspoons ground coriander
2 teaspoons ground cumin
10 fresh long green chillies, chopped coarsely
10 fresh small green chillies, chopped coarsely
1 large clove garlic, quartered
4 green onions, chopped coarsely
1 stick fresh lemon grass, sliced thinly
2 fresh kaffir lime leaves, sliced thinly
1 teaspoon finely chopped fresh galangal
1/4 cup coarsely chopped fresh coriander root
and stem mixture
1 teaspoon shrimp paste
1 tablespoon peanut oil

1 Stir ground coriander and cumin in small dry-heated frying pan over medium heat until fragrant.
2 Blend or process roasted spices with remaining ingredients, except for the oil, until mixture forms a paste, pausing to scrape down sides of machine occasionally during blending.
3 Add oil to paste mixture; continue to blend in machine or using mortar and pestle until smooth.

red curry paste
gaeng ped

PREPARATION TIME 20 MINUTES (PLUS STANDING TIME) COOKING TIME 3 MINUTES

20 dried long red chillies
1 teaspoon ground coriander
2 teaspoons ground cumin
1 teaspoon hot paprika
2 teaspoons finely chopped fresh ginger
3 large cloves garlic, quartered
1 medium (170g) red onion, chopped coarsely
2 sticks fresh lemon grass, sliced thinly
1 fresh kaffir lime leaf, sliced thinly
2 tablespoons coarsely chopped fresh coriander
root and stem mixture
2 teaspoons shrimp paste
1 tablespoon peanut oil

1 Place whole chillies in small heatproof jug, cover with boiling water; stand 15 minutes, drain.
2 Meanwhile, stir ground coriander, cumin and paprika over medium heat in small dry-heated frying pan until fragrant.
3 Blend or process chillies and roasted spices with remaining ingredients, except for the oil, until mixture forms a paste, pausing to scrape down sides of machine occasionally during blending.
4 Add oil to paste mixture; continue to blend in machine or using mortar and pestle until smooth.

curry pastes

121

massaman curry paste
gaeng masaman

PREPARATION TIME 15 MINUTES (PLUS STANDING TIME)
COOKING TIME 20 MINUTES

20 dried long red chillies
1 teaspoon ground coriander
2 teaspoons ground cumin
2 teaspoons ground cinnamon
1/2 teaspoon ground cardamom
1/2 teaspoon ground clove
5 large cloves garlic, quartered
1 large (200g) brown onion, chopped coarsely
2 sticks fresh lemon grass, sliced thinly
3 fresh kaffir lime leaves, sliced thinly
1 tablespoon coarsely chopped fresh ginger
2 teaspoons shrimp paste
1 tablespoon peanut oil

1 Preheat oven to moderate. Place chillies in small heatproof jug, cover with boiling water; stand 15 minutes, drain.
2 Meanwhile, combine ground coriander, cumin, cinnamon, cardamom and clove in small dry-heated frying pan; stir over medium heat until fragrant.
3 Place chillies and roasted spices in small shallow baking dish with remaining ingredients. Roast, uncovered, in moderate oven for 15 minutes.
4 Blend or process roasted curry paste mixture, or crush, using mortar and pestle, until smooth.

panang curry paste
gaeng panaeng

PREPARATION TIME 20 MINUTES (PLUS STANDING TIME)
COOKING TIME 3 MINUTES

25 dried long red chillies
1 teaspoon ground coriander
2 teaspoons ground cumin
2 large cloves garlic, quartered
8 spring onions, chopped coarsely
2 sticks fresh lemon grass, sliced thinly
2 teaspoons finely chopped fresh galangal
2 teaspoons shrimp paste
1/2 cup (75g) roasted unsalted peanuts
2 tablespoons peanut oil

1 Place chillies in small heatproof jug, cover with boiling water; stand 15 minutes, drain.
2 Meanwhile, stir ground coriander and cumin over medium heat in small dry-heated frying pan until fragrant.
3 Blend or process chillies and roasted spices with remaining ingredients, except for the oil, until mixture forms a paste, pausing to scrape down sides of machine occasionally during blending.
4 Add oil to paste mixture; continue to blend in machine or using mortar and pestle until smooth.

curry pastes

glossary

AUBERGINE also known as eggplant. Ranging in size from tiny to very large and in colour from pale green to deep purple, aubergine has an equally wide variety of flavours.

pea (makeua puong) slightly larger than a green pea and of similar shape and colour; sold fresh, in bunches like grapes, or pickled packed in jars. More bitter than the slightly larger thai aubergine, with which it can be substituted in many Thai recipes; both can be found in Asian grocery stores.

thai (makeua prao) golf-ball-sized aubergines available in different colours but most commonly green traced in off-white; crisper than the common purple Western variety, they have bitter seeds that must be removed before using.

BASIL

holy also known as kra pao or hot basil, is different from thai basil (horapa) and the familiar sweet basil used in Italian cooking; has an almost hot, spicy flavour similar to clove, and is used in cooking many Thai dishes, especially curries. Can be distinguished from horapa by the tiny 'hairs' on its leaves and stems.

thai also known as horapa, is different from holy basil and sweet basil in both look and taste. Having smaller leaves and purplish stems, it has a slight liquorice or aniseed taste, and is one of the basic flavours that typify Thai cuisine.

opal has large purple leaves and a sweet, almost gingery flavour. It can be used instead of thai but not holy basil in recipes.

BOK CHOY also known as bak choy, pak choi, chinese white cabbage or chinese chard, has a fresh, mild mustard taste; use stems and leaves, stir-fry or braise.

CHILLI

green generally unripened thai chillies but sometimes different naturally green varieties such as jalapeño or serrano chillies.

paste every Asian cuisine has its own chilli paste, and each is different from the next. We used a hot Vietnamese chilli paste in this book but you can use Indonesian sambal oelek (chilli with ginger, oil and garlic) or, for less heat, mild sweet thai chilli sauce, made with vinegar and sugar.

sauce if not specified as sweet, we used a hot Chinese variety made of chillies, soy and vinegar; use sparingly, increasing amounts to taste.

sweet chilli sauce Thai in origin, a comparatively mild, thin sauce made from red chillies, sugar, garlic and vinegar; used as a condiment more often than in cooking.

thai bright red to dark green in colour, ranging in size from small ('scuds') to long and thin; among the hottest of chillies.

CHINESE BARBECUED DUCK traditionally cooked in special ovens, this duck has a sweet-

sticky coating made from soy sauce, sherry, five-spice and hoisin sauce. It is available from Asian food stores.

CHINESE CABBAGE also known as peking or napa cabbage, wong bok or petsai. Elongated in shape with pale green, crinkly leaves, this is the most common cabbage in South-East Asia, forming the basis of the pickled Korean condiment, kim chi, and providing the crunch in vietnamese rice paper rolls. Can be shredded or chopped and eaten raw or braised, steamed or stir-fried.

CHIVES long, very fine green leaves usually eaten uncooked; related to the onion and leek, with subtle onion flavour.

flowering have rougher leaves than simple chives, with a teardrop-shaped pink bud at the top; used in salads or steamed and eaten as vegetable.

garlic also known as chinese chives; are strongly flavoured, have flat leaves and are eaten as a vegetable, usually in stir-fries.

CHOY SUM also known as pakaukeo or flowering cabbage, a member of the bok choy family; easy to identify with its long stems and yellow flowers. Can be eaten, stems and all, steamed or stir-fried.

COCONUT MILK/CREAM not the juice found inside the fruit, but liquid pressed from the white meat of a mature coconut. After

the liquid settles, the cream and 'milk' (thin white fluid) separate naturally. Coconut cream is obtained commercially from the first pressing of the coconut flesh alone, without the addition of water; the second pressing (less rich) is sold as the milk.

CORIANDER (pak chee) also known as cilantro; bright-green-leafed herb with a pungent flavour. Often stirred into a dish just before serving for maximum impact. The stems and roots are also used in Thai cooking; wash well before chopping.

CURRY PASTES

green the hottest of the traditional pastes; particularly good in chicken and vegetable curries, also in stir-fries and noodle dishes.

massaman has a spicy flavour reminiscent of Middle-Eastern cooking; favoured by southern Thai Muslim communities for use in hot stew-like curries and satay sauces.

panang based on the curries of Penang, an island off the north-west coast of Malaysia, close to the Thai border. A complex, sweet and milder variation of red curry paste; good with seafood and for adding to soups and salad dressings.

red probably the most popular curry paste; a hot blend of different flavours that complements the richness of pork, duck and seafood, also works well in marinades and sauces.

123

yellow one of the mildest pastes; similar to Indian curry due to use of yellow chillies and fresh turmeric. Good used with coconut in vegetable, rice and noodle dishes.

DRIED SHRIMP (goong hang) salted sun-dried prawns ranging in size from not much larger than a grain of rice to 'big' ones measuring about 1cm in length. They are sold packaged, shelled, in all Asian grocery stores.

FISH SAUCE called naam pla if it is Thai made; the Vietnamese version, nuoc naam, is almost identical. Made from pulverised salted fermented fish (usually anchovies); has a pungent smell and strong taste.

FRIED GARLIC (kratiem jiew) sold in Asian grocery stores packed in jars or in cellophane bags; used as a topping for various Thai rice and noodle dishes, and also as a condiment for a Thai meal.

GAI LARN (kanah) also known as gai lum, chinese broccoli or chinese kale; appreciated more for its stems than its coarse leaves. Can be served steamed and stir-fried, in soups and noodle dishes.

GALANGAL (ka) a rhizome with a hot ginger-citrusy flavour; used like ginger and garlic as a seasoning and as an ingredient. Sometimes known as thai or siamese ginger, it also comes in a dried powdered form called laos. Fresh ginger can be substituted but the flavour of the dish will not be the same.

pickled (ka dong) is used both in cooking and as a condiment. It is sold cryovac-packed or in jars in Asian grocery stores. You can substitute pickled ginger but the taste will not be exactly the same.

GREEN PAPAYA available in various sizes at many Asian shops and markets; look for one that is

very hard and slightly shiny. For use in Thai cooking, papaya must be totally unripe, the flesh so light green it is almost white. Buy the firmest one you can find; it will soften rapidly within a day or so.

KA CHAI sometimes spelled krachai or kah chi, also known as lesser galangal, chinese ginger or finger-root; long, brown fingerling-like roots available fresh, dried, canned or pickled in brine. Similar to ginger in flavour with a slight hint of camphor, it is found in Asian supermarkets and greengrocers.

KAFFIR LIME (magrood) also known as jeruk purut; bumpy-skinned, wrinkled green fruit of a small citrus tree originally grown in South Africa and South-East Asia. Its zest gives Thai food its unique aromatic flavour.

kaffir lime leaves (bai magrood) sold fresh, dried or frozen; look like two glossy dark green leaves joined end to end, forming a round hourglass shape. Dried leaves are less potent, so double the number called for in a recipe if you substitute dried for fresh leaves.

KECAP MANIS called sieu wan in Thai, sold under its Indonesian/ Malaysian name; dark, thick, sweet soy sauce used in most South-East Asian cooking. The soy's sweetness is derived from the addition of either molasses or palm sugar when brewed.

LEMON GRASS a tall, clumping, lemon-smelling and tasting, sharp-edged grass; the white lower part of the stem is used, finely chopped, in cooking.

MINT

thai (saranae) also known as marsh mint; similar to spearmint. Its somewhat thick round leaves are usually used raw, as a flavouring to be sprinkled over soups and salads.

vietnamese not a mint at all, but a pungent and peppery narrow-leafed member of the buckwheat family. It is also known as cambodian mint, pak pai (Thailand), laksa leaf (Indonesia) or daun kesom (Singapore). It is a common ingredient in Thai foods, particularly soups, salads and stir-fries.

MUSHROOMS

dried shitake have a unique meaty flavour. Sold dried; rehydrate before use.

oyster also known as abalone; grey-white mushrooms shaped like a fan. Prized for their smooth texture and subtle, oyster-like flavour.

shitake although cultivated, have the earthy taste of wild mushrooms. Large and fleshy, they are often used as a substitute for meat in some vegetarian dishes.

straw seldom available fresh but easily found canned or dried in Asian grocery stores. A common ingredient in stir-fries, they have an intense, earthy flavour.

NOODLES

bean thread (wun sen) made from extruded mung bean paste; also known as cellophane or glass noodles because they are transparent when cooked. White (not off-white like rice vermicelli), very delicate and fine; available dried in various-sized bundles. Must be soaked to soften before use; using them deep-fried requires no pre-soaking.

egg (ba mee) also known as yellow noodles; made from wheat flour and eggs, sold fresh or dried. Range in size from fine strands to wide pieces as thick as a shoelace.

fresh rice also known as ho fun, pho or kway tiau, depending on the country of manufacture. The most common form of noodles used in Thailand can be purchased

in various widths or in large sheets which are cut into the width noodle desired. Chewy and pure white, they do not need pre-cooking before use.

fried crispy egg noodles packaged already deep-fried.

hokkien also known as stir-fry noodles; fresh wheat flour noodles resembling yellow-brown thick spaghetti. Need no pre-cooking before use.

rice stick (sen lek) also known as ho fun or kway teow; especially popular South-East Asian dried rice noodles. Come in different widths – thin used in soups, wide in stir-fries – but all should be soaked in hot water until soft. Sen lek, the traditional noodles used in pad thai, measure about 5mm in width before they are soaked.

vermicelli (sen mee) also known as mei fun or bee hoon. These are used throughout Asia in spring rolls and cold salads; similar to bean thread but longer and made with rice flour instead of mung bean starch. Before using, soak the dried noodles in hot water until soft (about 15 minutes), then boil them briefly (from 1 to 3 minutes) and rinse with hot water. You can also deep-fry the dried noodles until crunchy for use in coleslaw, chinese chicken salad, as a garnish or as a bed for sauces.

OIL

peanut pressed from ground peanuts; most commonly used oil in Asian cooking because of its high smoke point (capacity to handle high heat without burning).

sesame made from roasted crushed white sesame seeds; used as a flavouring rather than a cooking medium.

vegetable any of a number of oils sourced from plants rather than animal fats.

PALM SUGAR (nam tan pip) also called jaggery, jawa or gula melaka; made from the sap of the sugar palm tree. Light brown to black in colour and usually sold in rock-hard cakes; substitute brown sugar if it is unavailable.

PAPRIKA ground dried red pepper (capsicum), available sweet or hot.

PATTYPAN SQUASH a round, slightly flat summer squash being yellow to pale green in colour and having a scalloped edge. Harvested young, it has firm white flesh and a distinct flavour.

PICKLED GARLIC (kratiem dong) sweet and subtle young green bulb, packed in jars whole and unpeeled in a vinegar brine. Eaten as a snack in Thailand; can also be used in cooking or served as a condiment for noodle or rice dishes.

PICKLED GREEN PEPPERCORNS (prik tai ahn) early-harvested unripe pepper that needs to be dried or pickled to avoid fermentation. We used pickled thai green peppercorns, which are canned, still strung in clusters, but you can use an equivalent weight from a bottle of green peppercorns in brine.

POMELO (som-o) similar to grapefruit but sweeter, somewhat more conical in shape and slightly larger, about the size of a small coconut. The firm rind peels away easily and neatly, like a mandarin, and the segments are easy to separate.

PRESERVED TURNIP (hua chai po or cu cai muoi on the label). Sold packaged whole or sliced, it is very salty and needs to be rinsed well before use.

RICE

black also known as purple rice because, while a deep charcoal in colour when raw, after cooking it turns a purplish-black colour. A medium-grain unmilled rice, with a white kernel under the black

bran, it has a nutty, whole-grain flavour and is crunchy to the bite, similarly to wild rice.

glutinous also known as 'sweet' rice or 'sticky' rice; a short, fat grain having a chalky white centre. When cooked, it becomes soft and sticky, hence the name; requires fairly long soaking and steaming times.

thai jasmine has a particular aromatic quality described as perfumed or floral; a long-grained white rice, it is sometimes substituted for basmati rice. Moist in texture, it clings together after cooking.

RICE PAPER also known as banh trang; different to the edible fine glossy paper used in the making of biscuits and confectionery. Made from rice paste and stamped into rounds; stores well at room temperature. Dipped momentarily in water to become pliable, it makes good wrappers for fried foods, spring rolls and uncooked vegetables.

SAMBAL OELEK (also ulek or olek) Indonesian in origin; a salty paste made from ground red chillies and vinegar.

SHALLOT

fried (homm jiew) are usually served as condiments on the Thai table or sprinkled over just-cooked dishes. Can be purchased packaged in jars or cellophane bags at all Asian grocery stores; once opened, they keep for months if stored tightly sealed. You can make your own by frying thinly sliced peeled shallots until golden-brown and crisp.

thai purple (homm) also called asian or pink shallots; used throughout South-East Asia, they are a member of the onion family but resemble garlic in that they grow in multiple-clove bulbs and are

intensely flavoured. They are eaten fresh or deep-fried as a condiment.

SHRIMP PASTE (kapi) also known as trasi or blanchan; it is a strong-scented, very firm preserved paste made of salted dried shrimp. Used as a pungent flavouring in many South-East Asian soups and sauces. Must be chopped or sliced thinly, then wrapped in foil and roasted before use.

SNAKE BEANS long (about 40cm), thin, round, fresh green beans, Asian in origin, with a taste similar to green or french beans. Used most frequently in stir-fries, they are also called yard-long beans because of their length.

SOY SAUCE (sieu) made from fermented soy beans. Several variations are available in most supermarkets and Asian food stores; everyday Thai cooking calls for the use of two of them: sieu wan (see kecap manis) or sieu dum (dark soy).

STAR ANISE a star-shaped dried pod whose seeds have an astringent aniseed flavour; used to flavour stocks and marinades.

TAMARIND from the same family as various beans, the tamarind tree is native to tropical Africa and, more recently, South-East Asia, and can grow as high as 25 metres. The tree produces clusters of brown 'hairy' pods (each of which is filled with seeds and a viscous pulp) that are dried and pressed into the blocks of tamarind found in Asian supermarkets. Gives a sweet-sour, slightly astringent taste to food. An important ingredient in Thai, Indian and other Asian cuisines, tamarind is used mainly as a souring agent in marinades, pastes, sauces and dressings. It is also used in the manufacturing of many curry pastes, ketchups and sauces.

tamarind concentrate (or paste) the commercial result of the distillation of tamarind juice into a condensed, compacted paste. Thick and purplish-black, it is ready to use, with no soaking or straining required; can be diluted with water according to taste. Use tamarind concentrate to add zing to sauces, chutneys and marinades.

TOFU (tao hu) also known as bean curd, an off-white, custard-like product made from the 'milk' of crushed soy beans; comes fresh as soft or firm, and processed as fried or pressed dried sheets. Leftover fresh tofu can be refrigerated in water (which is changed daily) up to 4 days. Silken tofu refers to the manufacturing method of straining the soy bean liquid through silk.

TURMERIC (kamin) a rhizome related to galangal and ginger; must be grated or pounded to release its somewhat acrid aroma and pungent flavour. Known for the golden colour it imparts to food, fresh turmeric can be substituted with the more common dried powder (use 2 teaspoons of ground turmeric plus 1 teaspoon of sugar for every 20g of fresh turmeric called for in a recipe).

VINEGAR

rice wine made from pure fermented rice with no flavourings added.

seasoned rice made from fermented rice, colourless and flavoured with sugar and salt.

WONTON WRAPPERS made of flour, eggs and water, they come in varying thicknesses. Sold packaged in large amounts and found in the refrigerated sections of Asian grocery stores; gow gee, egg or spring roll pastry sheets can be substituted. We used thin wrappers measuring 12cm x 12cm in this book.

conversion charts

MEASURES

The cup and spoon measurements used in this book are metric: one measuring cup holds approximately 250ml; one metric tablespoon holds 20ml; one metric teaspoon holds 5ml.

All cup and spoon measurements are level. The most accurate way of measuring dry ingredients is to weigh them. When measuring liquids, use a clear glass or plastic jug with metric markings.

We use large eggs with an average weight of 60g.

WARNING This book contains recipes for dishes made with raw or lightly cooked eggs. These should be avoided by vulnerable people such as pregnant and nursing mothers, invalids, the elderly, babies and young children.

DRY MEASURES

metric	imperial
15g	$^1/_2$oz
30g	1oz
60g	2oz
90g	3oz
125g	4oz ($^1/_4$lb)
155g	5oz
185g	6oz
220g	7oz
250g	8oz ($^1/_2$lb)
280g	9oz
315g	10oz
345g	11oz
375g	12oz ($^3/_4$lb)
410g	13oz
440g	14oz
470g	15oz
500g	16oz (1lb)
750g	24oz (1$^1/_2$lb)
1kg	32oz (2lb)

LIQUID MEASURES

metric	imperial
30ml	1 fl oz
60ml	2 fl oz
100ml	3 fl oz
125ml	4 fl oz
150ml	5 fl oz ($^1/_4$ pint/1 gill)
190ml	6 fl oz
250ml	8 fl oz
300ml	10 fl oz ($^1/_2$ pt)
500ml	16 fl oz
600ml	20 fl oz (1 pint)
1000ml (1 litre)	1$^3/_4$ pints

LENGTH MEASURES

metric	imperial
3mm	$^1/_8$in
6mm	$^1/_4$in
1cm	$^1/_2$in
2cm	$^3/_4$in
2.5cm	1in
5cm	2in
6cm	2$^1/_2$in
8cm	3in
10cm	4in
13cm	5in
15cm	6in
18cm	7in
20cm	8in
23cm	9in
25cm	10in
28cm	11in
30cm	12in (1ft)

OVEN TEMPERATURES

These oven temperatures are only a guide for conventional ovens. For fan-assisted ovens, check the manufacturer's manual.

	°C (Celcius)	°F (Fahrenheit)	gas mark
Very low	120	250	$^1/_2$
Low	150	275-300	1-2
Moderately low	170	325	3
Moderate	180	350-375	4-5
Moderately hot	200	400	6
Hot	220	425-450	7-8
Very hot	240	475	9

conversion charts

index